Charlton Laird, University of Nevada, Reno, Nevada. (credit, Ahmed Essa).

And Gladly Teche

Notes on Instructing the Natives in the Native Tongue

--◃{ **CHARLTON LAIRD** }▹--

Professor of English Emeritus
University of Nevada, Reno

Prentice-Hall, Inc. *Englewood Cliffs, N.J.*

Library of Congress Catalog Card No.:
72–135651

Current printing (last number):
10 9 8 7 6 5 4 3

Printed in the United States of America

PRENTICE-HALL INTERNATIONAL, INC., *London*
PRENTICE-HALL OF AUSTRALIA, PTY. LTD., *Sydney*
PRENTICE-HALL OF CANADA, LTD., *Toronto*
PRENTICE-HALL OF INDIA PRIVATE LIMITED, *New Delhi*
PRENTICE-HALL OF JAPAN, INC., *Tokyo*

And gladly wolde he lerne and gladly teche.

GEOFFREY CHAUCER

Addressing a combined meeting of teachers, writers, and publisher's representatives (see p. 216), I observed ". . . Editors have given me words, sentences, whole paragraphs; they did not even expect to be thanked, and they have never stolen anything." Following are the names of some of the editors of whom I was thinking; to them and their colleagues in a little-sung profession I am happy to dedicate this book:

Helene Laird	Paul O'Connell
David B. Guralnik	Cecil Yarbrough
William A. Pullin	Robb Heinemann
Dudley Cloud	Richard T. Congdon
Richard L. Nelson	Ronald Campbell
Robert L. Page	Gray Williams
David Keightley	Richard Marek
Donald Hammonds	William H. Oliver

Introduction

Good teachers are good teachers because they have brains, great learning, engaging personalities, and enough experience to learn what to do with themselves. This observation on teachers and teaching appears in a lecture in this collection but it might better be applied to Professor Laird's own long-time love affair with teachers of English in our schools and colleges.

Long before large numbers of scholars began to interest themselves in the quality of instruction in the lower school or even the lower division of our universities, Charlton Laird was thoughtfully, persistently, and willingly providing insights and encouragement to those responsible for guiding the language development of our youth. (One lecture in this collection was first presented in the Thirties, and several predate the content-centered curriculum reform efforts initiated during the Fifties.) Thus Professor Laird's career spans the entire era of self-inquisition that the profession has undertaken during the past twenty years, and he possesses the ability to see in totality the entire field of English. This interest is language, not grammar or semantics in isolation. He limits himself not to any one school of theorists, but engages with syntactics, semantics, psychology of language, with people using language, learning it, and teaching it.

But if many occasions which time and again brought teachers clamoring for Professor Laird's reflections have long since receded in memory, the ideas which emerged out of these occasions have a timeless vitality of their own. Here is Laird on language and its uses, on writing and reading, on new rhetorics and the old, on literature as an integrative force in the education of the young. Here is Laird on the strengths and weaknesses in all aspects of English teaching. Here, too, is Laird gently reminding all teachers that they not lose sight of the broad outline of what they are doing and why they are doing it.

Precisely because Professor Laird never loses his own perspective, his observations on the nature of English and its teaching in the classroom retain a continuing value and pertinence. Note, for instance, his concern for students assuming responsibility to formulate their own questions, teaching one another, originating projects, working in panels. A man like Laird, devoting himself in a broad humane way to language and to learning, does not go out of style like the special scholar with narrow interests who may identify himself for a time with a particular issue or point of view. Teachers who have been privileged to work closely with him will be delighted to find that the kindly quiet charm which pervades his personal teaching continually enlivens his prose. Those guided by the routine rhetoric of convention speeches will be impressed by the liveliness of expression in this collection.

When I first met Charlton Laird well over a decade ago, I regarded him primarily as a distinguished college instructor and as a well known author of interesting, popular books. I have long since discovered in addition that he is a sensible observer of things English; a wise and humane individual who in his unstinting efforts to improve the teaching of English has honored the entire profession. Now that Professor Laird's lectures are available for all teachers of English, an even greater number of teacher-readers will come to know him as a good teacher—a teacher with brains, great learning, and engaging personality, and, above all, enough experience to have learned what to do with himself.

James R. Squire
Lincoln, Massachusetts

Foreword

There are a few hundred of us; a few thousand if you count the apprentices, the occasional recruits, the one-session wonders. We are the anonymous engineers of language learning, both mundane and artistic language learning, as little known outside our convoluting circles as are the engineers who control the resilience of plastics and direct the private lives of rockets. Some few of us become known for something else; any engineer of learning may incidentally be a scholar, an author, a college president, an authority on jazz music; but for what we have in common we are generally unknown.

Ostensibly we are teachers of English, and numerically most of us are or have been teachers, from kindergarten into graduate school, but few of us are teachers and only teachers. We are publisher's editors and salesmen, trainers of prospective pedagogues, devisers of classroom devices, curriculum planners and supervisers, departmental executives, writers of textbooks. Our ranks are uncommonly open; almost anyone is welcome, but few can offer the curious combination of dogged patience and indifference to personal gain, of tough and resilient intelligence, of delicately blended idealism and good sense that is apparently the uncoded prerequisite of admission beyond the outer sanctum. Few of us think of ourselves as belonging to anything, except that most of us have some sort of professional affiliation, but we are all involved, as though involvement were the religion of our cult.

We have our annual rites and ceremonies; every year we can be found at meetings: of the National Council of Teachers of English, of the College Conference on Composition and Communication, The Conference on English Education, the College English Association, and the like. Here old acquaintances are renewed and the recruits surveyed, curricula and methods are debated, published textbooks are promoted and new books planned and contracted for, papers read and argued about. Then, after a few days, the few hundred engineers of language learning, along with the thousands who have come to see and hear them, go back to wherever they came from and the year's ritual is over. The effects are not over; the impact of any meeting of what most English teachers refer to as "the National Council" will be felt among hundreds of publishing houses and suppliers of classroom materials, in thousands of school systems, and among millions of students. And most of what happens at such conventions hinges upon the few hundred people whom I have called engineers of language learning.

The role of these people can be readily undervalued, and usually it is. Everyone knows his native language, at least well enough to use it, and he is likely to have little notion of how much more he would need to know if he were to teach it well. We tend to forget, since language is common as air and water, that the three R's are still the basis of education, and that two of them are what is commonly called English and I have called language learning. We are now coming to realize that without good air and water we are not likely to thrive physically, and somewhat less practically we are learning that without good use of language a complex society is not likely to prosper mentally and socially.

Even less are we aware that knowing about composition, language, and literature are not enough. A writer like Henry L. Mencken and a scholar like Hans Kurath may greatly enhance our understanding of American dialects, but if we are to use dialectology to discourage rioting in the ghettos—and many believe we can do more with language than with mace and night sticks—the knowledge of dialects must become a working way of life in the classroom, where the results will be better or worse depending upon the teacher's grasp and the excellence or crudity of the tools with which he works. Similarly, a culture like ours rests upon thinking, and most brains work through language; the better the command of language, the better the thought and the more there is of it. But how can one improve another's grasp of language? It is extremely difficult. More and more our society rests upon communication, but what can be done about the fact? McLuhan has told us how important communication is, but he would doubtless be the first to agree that no single human being has ever been able to do much about it at the working level, and few but the experts know even how to begin intelligently. Thus when I call these people engineers and admit that most of them are but little known, I am far from belittling them or the need for them. Science cannot become operative without technology; technology is impossible without engineers. In the end, language learning may be the most important study; of the intellectual skills it is the most widely disseminated and perhaps the most in need of deliberate dissemination; and at the engineering level, such dissemination is extremely difficult.

The papers collected here are representative of the sort of thing that can be heard when the engineers of language learning and their fellows convene, at conventions, institutes, and the like. Inevitably, the papers themselves reflect the impact of the audiences for which they were written, and these are disparate. Some few auditors may know the speaker and his work; they comprehend his subject as well as he does, perhaps better, but they have come on the chance he may have something fresh to say. A few more will be personal friends, tinged with the essence of martyrdom, noble souls who have learned that he also serves who, hearing last year's speech warmed over, only sits and suffers. The speaker is aware of these fellow engineers, but he is aware also that he can do little for them; whatever he has for their ears must wait until he and they can meet elsewhere over convivial glasses.

For the speaker knows that this meeting was not planned for specialists. Even if it is a national meeting, it convenes in some place, and the audience will be mainly local—people who did not hear the same speaker when he appeared last year and the year before. Most teachers cannot afford, in time or money, to fly to Seattle for one meeting, to Boston for another, to Miami Beach, and then to Honolulu. If the average teacher manages to attend a national convention every half dozen years or so, seizing the occasion when the language engineers meet in the vicinity, he is doing very well. It is for these practicing teachers, primarily, that the meeting has been convened. As for the engineers, who may do most of the public talking, they can always find ways of communicating with one another. What the audience at such a convention mainly wants is not so much the findings of the year, but a digest of the best that has come out of the last decade or so. They have come hoping to be professionally rejuvenated, to be moved to new and better teaching, and, greatly to the credit of such organizations as the National Council and its subsidiaries, that is often what happens. But it happens in part because speakers understand that they had best repeat in Atlanta some of what they said the previous year in Denver and the year before that in Chicago. Thus such a speaker—and here is the pertinence of these observations for the collection in hand—while he always tries to bring in something new, finds himself seduced into what Falstaff called "damnable iteration," an activity which the inimitable braggart considered well calculated to corrupt a saint.

I have not been able to expunge all of this repetition; it was incorporated deliberately, and while I would now willingly remove it, I find that some repetition is so woven into the texture of the prose that I have difficulty unravelling it. From the general reader I can only beg indulgence; as for the students, I can solace myself with the ancient maxim that anything to be taught should be repeated at least seven times. Presumably it need not be written seven times, but I trust I have reduced the iteration quotient below that level.

One might add that otherwise the papers have been left pretty much as they were written. They have been excised for brevity and the reduction of tautology; since they were delivered over the course of thirty years, they have been cut, also, to remove topical material no longer pertinent. They were mostly written, but written to be read, so that they retain a colloquial quality which I would have considered inappropriate if they had been composed as essays. I have not tried to change this style, since I conceived that a degree of familiarity may be welcome to teachers and prospective teachers accustomed to being lectured at.

The whole collection may warrant some apology, from both the author and the publisher. So far as I know, no one of my colleagues has ever presumed to collect and print samples of his chattings to the profession, not even under the pleas that, for nostalgic reasons, some practitioners may care to have a sample of professional papers collected from the desk drawers and the arcane journals that are the accustomed final resting place of such effusions, and that some prospective teachers may welcome a reprinting of admonitions delivered when they themselves were too young to know or too nonchalant to care. As for the general public, the papers may have some interest as a sort of Americana, evidence of fauna not so exotic as those explored by skindivers, but exotic enough to suggest life out of a strange and in some ways foreign element, the record of creatures for whom language is a profession as well as a medium.

Contents

And Gladly Teche

A No-Position Paper
on Teaching Language

The following was prepared as a self-introduction before a workshop concerning the teaching of language in
the secondary schools, held in conjunction with the convention of the National Council of Teachers of English
in Houston, 1966. It has not previously been published.

I have been asked to write a position paper, but since I am not sure I have any "position" so far as the teaching of English in the secondary school is concerned, I am somewhat at a loss. I have no ninety-five propositions to tack on anybody's church door. As I see the teaching of English in our time, positions are less important than things to be done, aims to be furthered, and possible means of furthering them.

This is not to say we have no reason to meet in Houston, nor that I shall not be violent here—I fear I usually am. For if I have nothing I think of as a position, I presume I have a sort of posture. I have long felt that teaching the use of the native language to the native users is about the most important thing that any human being can do for another, and I was long grieved that so much teaching of what was called English was frequently so trivial. Accordingly, I have been greatly heartened, since in recent years we have been experiencing something that partakes at once of a tremendous upsurge, a revolution, and a rededication. I assume this was the intent of the meeting last year in Boston, that it is the purpose of the meeting this year in Houston, and that it will be the hope of the meeting next year in Honolulu to further the upsurge, to help direct the rededication. But in the conventional sense, this posture of mine should probably not be called a "position," at least not to the extent that it is controversial. If I say that I believe in more and better teaching of English, I do not expect anyone who comes to Houston to rise up and assert that he believes in less and worse teaching of English. If that is what he wants, he is likely to stay home, and I shall be left defending a position—however impregnable—against no assault.

Thus if I have anything that could be called a position it is perhaps this: that we should not lose sight of the broad outlines of what we are doing and why we are doing it. Teachers sometimes act as though they assume that their job is to teach grammar, or to teach literature, or to teach English 11, whereas I trust that our job is to teach the use of language, and that grammar or English 11 are the means and tools with which we teach. Fortunately, I believe we do now have a better understanding of what our business is, and we have a better grasp, also, of the tools we can use.

Part of our difficulty, I surmise, grows from a confusion on our workbench, an uncertainty as how we should classify our tools. We tell ourselves that the language arts are reading, writing, speaking, and listening. At the same time we tell ourselves, (or at least we organize our courses as though we had told ourselves,) that we are teaching literature, composition, and speech; and I have the feeling that not always do our courses reflect a well-ordered reconciliation of the various skills with the understanding we profess.

Fundamental here, I assume, is that we should know what it is our business to teach and what we need not teach, and I seem to observe that this distinction is unusually important in language. Most language is learned naturally and unconsciously. Such learning is probably best. At least it is the least painful, and it is probably the most economical, as those people can attest who have tried to learn a foreign language by conscious methods. Accordingly we have been telling ourselves for years that a young child knows all basic grammar by the age of five or six, and this is presumably true, but we have been less concerned with asking ourselves the corollary question—what do we need to teach the child that he will not learn by himself? That, after all, is our professional job.

—⋈ 2. ⊱—

The New Ten Commandments for Teachers of Composition

The following decalogue was prepared for the Idaho Conference of the Teachers of English; read in Boise, it was repeated for teachers in Toronto, Canada, and variously pillaged elsewhere. It is certainly not infallible, eternal, or divine. We are told that the original decalogue appeared on "two tables of stone, written with the finger of God." I am sure these commandments have nothing of the permanence suggested by stone, and they were probably not written with anyone's finger, certainly not with the Lord's; I rather suspect a battered typewriter in my office of having been the scriptural agent. There are other evidences that these admonitions are apocryphal; they are positive, not negative, telling what should be done, whereas the genuine decalogue is mainly composed of thou-shalt-nots. The fact is that the author does not know what should not happen in high school, since he has never taught there, but he has taught a good many college students to whom something should have happened that did not. From those observations of widespread inadequacy, the decalogue has grown; it has not been previously published.

—◦◖ 1. *Thou shalt have no gods before me:* Teaching the use of the native language includes teaching the use of the human mind, a means with which the mind works, and the greatest tool that mankind has ever devised. Teachers of English have the right to believe that in professing the native language they have the opportunity of performing for other human beings a service so important that few men or women ever have the means of doing so much for one another. They should teach with the devotion and zeal that their calling warrants.

2. *Thou shalt rise above adultery:* You should not adulterate your teaching; you should teach over your students' heads, not under their feet. Students should be taught to write and speak as they cannot yet write and speak, not to avoid errors by trying to compose like morons. Some teachers are tempted to instruct their charges to write like small children, in order that they will make no mistakes, but this is the pedagogical sin of sins: to teach the student what he knows already, not what he needs to know. Any young person who produces a composition without error is not trying to do enough; he should be attempting structures which as yet he cannot control, seeking words he does not as yet command, not writing dull sentences to avoid fragments.

3. *Thou shalt bear true witness:* Students should come to understand that one of the worst crimes man can commit against the language is to use it to say nothing. They should learn that writing is saying something and good writing is saying much, cramming a sentence with detail and toughening the structure that carries this detail. Strengthening prose is worth the effort, both for the prose and for the mind that labors with it.

4. *Thou shalt honor thy father, Thought, and thy mother, Language:* You should teach composition as the working of the mind, trying to penetrate to the nature of learning, helping others

5

learn to love and know words, their beauty and subtlety and power.

5. *Thou shalt teach composition as a means of life:* You should teach paragraphs as discipline of the mind, as means of developing and ordering thought and expression; you should teach sentences as devices for ordering ideas, sophisticated sentence patterns as the instrument of adult communication; you should teach the nature of meaning and the choice of words as the embodiment of thought and reality.

6. *Thou shalt make thy students write and thou shalt do to thyself what thou dost to others:* Writing can be improved by reading, by analyzing written work, and by many other means, but writing is a skill, albeit an intellectual skill. To learn writing, one must write, and write, and rewrite; you should make your students write and you should take your own assignments. How can you teach writing if you have never seriously tried to learn it yourself?

7. *Thou shalt promote life by teaching writing as art:* All writing is to a degree creative, and this commandment is a positive phrasing of the old commandment, "Thou shalt not kill." The urge to create is one of the closest links to the divine; it should be encouraged by attempting creative writing. And as in the previous commandment, thou shalt take thine own assignment; how can you teach creativity unless you, yourself, seriously endeavor to create?

8. *Thou shalt teach thy students not to steal:* Students should learn to respect intellectual property and intellectual integrity, and they should learn the means of embodying this respect in their thinking and writing; they should learn to deal objectively with the writing of others, and they should master the techniques by which a writer makes known his awareness of the uncertainty and mystery of a world in which fact is always shot through with error, in which truth is always qualified.

9. *Thou shalt have no false gods:* You should teach spelling, punctuation, and capitalization, along with mechanics and usage generally, as the conveniences and minor virtues they are—of the earth, earthy—for salvation is not in them. They should be taught, and taught well, as devices with which to clarify meaning and to observe the etiquette of mentally cultured people, but they are not divine and they should not be taught as the holy of holies.

10. *Thou shalt remember the Sabbath and keep it holy:* By the

Sabbath is meant whatever time you reserve out of each week to renew yourself, to read, to think, to do research, to write. This is the most precious time in any week, the most important time for the teacher as a teacher. It must be kept inviolate. We teach out of the wealth of our knowledge and the abundance of our enthusiasm, not out of our ignorance and our dullness. We owe it to our students and our communities to be living examples of literate use of language. Your administration should understand these matters, that you need time to be a professional, creative person, and should allow you time for this, but if your school does not allow you time, take it. If something must suffer, let the routine suffer. As a doctor's primary responsibility is to his patient, as a lawyer's is to his client, so, as a professional person your primary reponsibility is to your students and to yourself in keeping fit to serve your students. You owe loyalty to the school system that employs you, but it is a secondary loyalty. One should perhaps add that when teachers are granted a Sabbath for intellectual renewal and mental growth they should use it that way; not all do.

It is written that on the occasion of the announcement of the original decalogue, "All the people saw the thunderings, and the lightnings, and the noise of the trumpet, and the mountain smoking, and when the people saw it, they removed, and stood afar off." The annunciation of this new decalogue has been accompanied by no such demonstrations, and such pyrotechnics are probably not to be expected; nor is the announcement likely to be venerated by "all the people." This is perhaps another reason to suspect these commandments of being apocryphal, but they have at least this much similarity with the earlier statement, that most of the people who do hear them are likely to stand "afar off."

—❧ 3. ☙—

A Teacher of Literature
Must Be

The previous papers concern language and composition. The following statement was written at the request of the Conference on English Education and was read before a session of the conference at the University of Colorado, 1968, on the preparation appropriate for a teacher of literature.

Teaching the Teacher of English, part 2, ed. Oscar H. Haugh (Champaign, Ill.: National Council of Teachers, 1968) pp. 1–4.

8

A good teacher of literature resembles a poem at least in this, that however much he means, mainly he must be. This is not at all to imply that such teachers cannot or need not be taught. Quite the contrary; but it is to suggest that in part good teachers are born, and insofar as they are made they are made best by being developed, not by being provided with things to say or methods to be applied. If I seem here to be belittling the teaching of teachers let me abjure any such heresy at once; I am convinced that all good teachers have been developed, however good the initial teacher material, by good formal instruction or by intelligent self-discipline, and usually and probably inevitably by both.

I should perhaps acknowledge at this point that I am aware that the selection of potential teachers of literature is not our subject this morning, and I hope I am myself enough of an English teacher to recognize the virtue of having a subject and sticking to it. This one diversion seems to me useful, however, to avoid misunderstanding, particularly since I shall be talking more about people than material. Not always do school boards, or administrators, or even the teachers themselves recognize that good teachers are in part inherently good teachers. Based upon a witticism, the notion is common that anyone who cannot do can teach. I trust that you and I know better, and accordingly I shall not argue the point, although I could, and could also point out that many doers cannot teach, but wish they could. I desire merely to extend this line of thinking and to point out that good teachers are people with distinctive qualities, and that teachers of literature need particular, unusual, and generally admirable qualities. This insight into human nature need not surprise us. We are all aware that a good teacher of doctoral candidates in nuclear physics might not make a good teacher of pre-school morons, and vice versa. We are familiar with the fact that good students of English may not do well in mathe-

9

matics or baton twirling, and we have tended to be a bit apologetic on this account, as though science and technology, home economics and range management are the only virtues. We need not belittle ourselves. We may honestly maintain that the qualities which go to make good teachers of literature are highly admirable virtues, virtues not commonly possessed, virtues that may properly be treasured.

Now I come to my point. Good teachers of literature are those who have great potential as teachers, and as specialists in literature, and in whom these potentialities have been developed. Preparing a teacher of literature, then, is encouraging such a person to be. The problem in educating a teacher of literature is not so much providing him with something he should know as it is helping him to become.

I am aware that in making such a pronouncement I am uttering what many will consider heresy. It is not the philosophy embodied in most departments at the collegiate or at any other level, although a considerable number of teachers and administrators who would not be able to implement this principle would accept it in the abstract. I must now ask what a good teacher of literature should be, and here I anticipate even less agreement. First and foremost, I should say he must be a lover of literature. The initial objection here may be that not everyone can love literature. This I should immediately acknowledge, just as I would admit that not everyone can love cats, accounting, or the binomial theorem, but that is just another way of saying that not everyone should be given the privilege of teaching literature, and to me it is a great privilege. Within limits love of literature usually grows from experience with literature, from understanding and from what we rather vaguely call appreciation. This is not easy to teach. Teaching students the names of Shakespeare's plays and the birth and death dates of the author is much easier for both the teacher and the taught than teaching the subtlety and pervading tragedy of *Hamlet*. True love of literature, like true love of anything, can be taught only indirectly. The direct approach, "Isn't it beautiful?" is not more likely to inculcate love of literature than the commensurate question, "Why can't you behave?" is likely to instill moral virtue. Fortunately, love of art and language are infectious. They can be taught to those who are teachable, if we keep firmly before us the conviction that we are teaching the love of literature, not the secondary facts about literature. If we are endeavoring to teach love of literature, very wide reading in literature is likely to do more good than any amount of reading about literature.

Second, I should say that a good teacher of literature must be able to read. Here I am thinking of several sorts of reading. Presumably a teacher of literature should be able to read rapidly in order to read widely, but even more important he must be able to read accurately, with perception and penetration. Many professed teachers of literature cannot read at all in this sense; they cannot penetrate to what an adult writer is saying overtly, not to mention sensing what a poet endeavors to suggest. A teacher of literature should be able to read orally, and the younger the students the more important oral reading is. Most students at any level can sense literature only if it is read well to them, and this is true particularly of poetry and drama, but it is true, although to a lesser degree, of truly great passages of prose, either fiction or nonfiction. Of course a teacher can get some help here; we now have many records of modern poets reading their own works and of skilled interpreters reading the classics. We can scarcely expect that all English teachers will be able to read Chaucer with ease and comfort, but if they cannot they had best play records. Chaucer wrote mellifluous poetry, and to read him as though he is a labor, even a labor of love, is scarcely a service to anyone. Teachers can profit from better readers than they, and from readers who have special qualifications for certain sorts of reading, the reading of plays, for example, through a number of voices, but all the audial devices in the world will not make a good teacher of literature. He must be something more than the operator of a tape player; he must have learned to read, and his education should be calculated to help him as a reader.

The good teacher of literature should have had experience with his subject as a creator. That is, he should have tried to write, and the more different sorts of writing he has tried the better. I am not here saying that a good teacher of literature must be a good novelist or poet or playwright. No doubt that would help, but there are many good teachers who could never be good practicing literary artists and many good writers who would be bad teachers. But to understand the written word the teacher must understand writing, and to understand writing he must have faced blank paper and have wrestled with it. Pretty obviously, having children helps women to become good mothers, and every teacher knows that no number of courses in pedagogy can entirely replace classroom experience. To know writing one must try to write, however bad the result; every teacher of literature needs it for his own well-rounded approach to his job. He needs it, also, because students should attempt creative writing, however inept the products, and at a minimum a teacher should have seriously tried what he endeavors to teach.

A good teacher of literature has other skills and virtues, but partly in the interests of time I shall mention only the most important of these, and relatively lightly. A good teacher should be able to explicate; he should be literate enough so that he can help students formulate their own thoughts by joining the students in the process of clarifying emergent ideas. Thus training in the principles and practice of criticism is important for teachers of literature, particularly if, in learning to explicate, the teacher learns to restrain his practice of it. Talking about literature, even about literary art, should never displace, as it often does, the experience of literature itself. In a sense which Shakespeare probably never intended, the play's the thing, and so is the novel or the poem.

The good teacher of literature should be so well informed that he can branch out from any given work or body of literature to other related pieces. The knowledge of works as different as James Joyce's *Ulysses* and the Norse *Saga of Burnt Njal* can both contribute to the teaching of a short story like Hemingway's *Ten Little Indians*. A teacher of literature should be able, almost spontaneously, to suggest that there is no end to what Keats called "the realms of gold," that no matter how far the student goes good things will always rise before him.

The teacher of literature should have experienced language, which is at once his tool and the tool of those who wrote what he professes. Personally, I do not see how anyone who loves either language or literature can be indifferent to the other, but if the teacher does not find language exciting, at least he can know something about it and be able to use it. He should, for example, be able to write a paragraph, and too few teachers can. He should have a working knowledge of at least one foreign language; for these purposes languages closely linked to English, like French and Latin, have advantages, but tongues that are not even descended from Indo-European, like Chinese and Menominee also have their uses. He should understand the nature and working of language, and for most teachers this would mean a minimum of one course in historical and one in modern linguistics, or commensurate private reading. Of course such insight should grow almost automatically from a comparison of a foreign with the native language, but as foreign languages are at present taught in this country, an understanding of the nature of language does not usually follow.

A teacher of literature should be sufficiently broad in background and philosophic in bent to see before and after, both in time and culture. The teacher should be able to relate literature to the life from which it has sprung, to the principles of art with which it is instinct. A teacher of literature can never know enough, but at a minimum he should have a grasp of the major principles of science and an introduction to the study of man in his environment. Of these last I should personally say that the most important are anthropology and psychology, although history, philosophy, economics, political science, sociology and other studies have their uses as well.

A good teacher should know about literature and be able to employ the results of literary scholarship and criticism. Knowing something of what the Romantic Movement was in England helps us penetrate to meaning and sense the emotion in the *Ode on Intimations of Immortality*—and even in the Lucy poems—which we might miss otherwise. Knowing that Faulkner raised mules and that Lamb was a little sprite of a man who stuttered may not be crucial, but even such details help understand the men and what they did. The facts of literary history have their uses, even though these uses are secondary in teaching. The difficulty arises when, as extensively in the past and far too commonly today, the circumstances of literature are confused with literature itself.

In summary, I might observe that being, as I conceive being for the teacher of literature, is not easy, and cultivating this being is not easy, either; but in my view the training of teachers of literature should be directed primarily to that end.

◂◃ 4. ▹▸

Language:
Relevance and Irrelevance,
or How to Suffer
from Hallucination

The following lecture, prepared at the request of the committee planning the first meeting of the Western Conference for Teachers of English, was read in Las Vegas, March, 1970, where a convention was considering the theme, "English Teaching Today and Tomorrow: Relevance or Irrelevance." I fear my paper was not what the committee had in mind.

It reflects my personal ambivalence when I have observed demands that education be relevant, an end which I have long applauded in the abstract, although I have seen it supported in ways seemingly irrelevant. Some of those who have preferred charges against modern education have assumed that once the charge was made, the defendant was adjudged guilty, that no evidence was needed. When evidence was submitted it seemed not always to confirm that modern teaching is irrelevant, but rather that many students are seeking, and not finding quick cures for immediate practical troubles, particularly those involving social problems. Education leading to immediate solutions has its uses, but I must believe it has only limited uses, and that much education must be long-term,

14

calculated to gain its ends by cultivating minds, not mainly by convicting social culprits and overthrowing institutions.

But that is not the reason we elected to reprint the lecture here. In the course of trying to explain my position I seem to have been able to phrase more generally than on some occasions what I have to say about language, and consequently the piece may serve as a sort of introduction to the next half dozen or so papers. It is the most recent of the lectures, prepared while the book itself was being edited.

As you will know, I have been asked to consider the problem of how the teaching of language can be made relevant, but first I have the more immediate problem of making this speech relevant. Here I find I must take cognizance of a disease that has been moving through our school systems, which I shall call *logophobia,* fear of words or a word. The symptoms of this affliction are many and insidious; they include susceptibility to guilt complexes, inability to distinguish between fact and fancy, and general deterioration of the critical faculties. If I have dreamed up the name for this disease, let me assure you I have not concocted the disease itself. At times it has become epidemic, sweeping the country; during the McCarthy era, for example, words like *communist* and *communism* so infected American good sense that we were years coming to recognize that communism within the country posed no serious threat to our democratic institutions and that men and women who insist on using their own minds are not *per se* insidious or subversive. The present outbreak has been more restricted. Being largely limited to our educational systems, and to those persons involved with them, it springs from dread of the word *relevant,* and other terms associated with it. The result has been that we as teachers and administrators have tended to panic whenever anyone has shouted the word *relevant* at us, whether or not the word was used advisedly.

Some of this phobia is justified. After all, the word *relevant,* for whatever reasons, has been associated with the burning of public buildings, violent uprisings and the closing of schools and universities, and the resort to guns and tear gas in the streets. On the other hand, the use of the word itself has arisen in part from several other diseases, which should be treated for themselves, and not allowed to contribute to the spread of logophobia among teachers, parents, administrators, and students. I refer to two aberrations which I shall call *noosphobia* and *theriaphobia,* respectively, fear

16

of using the mind and fear of becoming a student. As for the first, fear of using the mind, it accounts for part of the demand for relevance in teaching. I have never been able to give a course but that some students, and often many students, tried to make it less relevant than I thought it should be. For me, the most relevant courses are those that teach students to use their minds. . . . [The explication of the other coined word, theriaphobia, led me rather far afield; perhaps that bit of persiflage can be omitted.]

Now if we are back to words like *relevance* and *irrelevance,* and they do not mean much as they are often being used these days, they are pertinent when they are used about something—language, and for somebody—our students. Even here, however, I must add one more modest reservation. We are asked to consider how we, as teachers, can make language relevant. I cannot refrain from asserting that it is already relevant, and that we cannot keep the study of language from being relevant for all human minds, could not help it if we tried. Language, especially the native language, is the basic means of communication for most human beings; for most minds, it is the single most useful tool to aid thinking. No man, or no woman, ever learns to use it as well as he might, nor well enough to afford him the greatest advantage and pleasure. By its nature, the study of language is inherently relevant for everybody, but that does not mean that problems of relevance do not rise in connection with it: some aspects of language study may be more relevant than others, particularly with various individuals and at various times and places, and language teaching can be more or less relevant. Thus I suspect that our supposed question, how can we make the teaching of language relevant, breaks down into several somewhat related questions: Do we need to stimulate students by helping them to see that the study of language is relevant? How can we make our teaching of language more relevant, granted our students and their particular needs? And although language as a study is inherently relevant, are we in fact teaching language, or very much of it?

I shall elect to consider the last question first, since for my responsibilities in this program, it seems to offer more than do some of the others. Are we teaching language? Nominally, the answer is easy. We teach language, and we have long intended to teach language; until recently we called our elementary schools grammar schools, as though grammar was the principal subject to be taught therein. That in using this term we were permitting ourselves to be the victims of an amusing semantic shift need not concern us here; the fact remains that grammar is an important part of language, that the school systems were organized in part on the theory that teaching grammar was their business, and that the public generally has assumed that grammar, along with spelling, penmanship, reading, and writing should be, and is being taught in the schools.

Only recently have we begun to understand that statements like these seem to imply more than actually they do. Consider grammar. Most schools teach no grammar at all, or at least very little, if one defines grammar as the ways languages work, or as the way a given language works. Schools have taught usage and called it grammar, and whereas no sharp line can be drawn between grammar and usage—there are few sharp lines anywhere in language study—the principles through which a language functions and the etiquette approved for certain dialects within a language are by no means the same. In a large way, the difference is apparent and quite real. Insofar as grammar was taught, until recently, it was not the grammar of modern English, whatever it was, and was so inadequate that if a youngster had known no more grammar than appeared in his grammar books he could never have either used or comprehended the language. As for other aspects of language, penmanship and spelling are useful skills, but relatively minor ones. Reading and writing are of course basic and essential, but on the whole they have been meagerly taught; most Americans now learn to sign their names and write simple sentences, to read advertisements and the more popular newspapers and magazines, but few of our young people attempt literate conversation, learn to produce precise and vigorous prose, or are able to understand such prose if they encounter it. Not many school systems consistently remind their students that such competence in the language is their business, or have been in a position to give the student much help if he should ask for it. As we all know, most students have been graduated, and are still being graduated, without any real understanding of what language is, how it works, or what is its importance in modern society.

Now we might notice that although the study of the native language is relevant for all users of the language, not all aspects of this study are equally relevant for everybody. Obviously, you and I should study grammar; if we are to profess the use of the native language we should understand that language well, and both a broad understanding of grammatical possibilities and the peculiarities of given languages are imperative for us. On the other hand, we all learned some time ago that what has conventionally been taught as English grammar did not do much to help young people produce literate prose. How relevant such concepts as transformation, stratification, and tagmemics may be is still very uncertain; they are certainly relevant for all serious students of language, are probably relevant for most teachers of English, but are probably not relevant, in the present state of our knowledge, for ghetto six year-olds.

Or consider usage. A recent desk dictionary is very proud of what it calls its Usage Panel. Presented with a locution like "She invited John and myself," more than ninety-five percent of the panel condemned it; Professor Gilbert Highet called it "a prissy evasion," and the sports columnist Walter Smith said it is "the refuge of idiots taught early that *me* is a dirty word." This is a very common usage; although ninety-five percent of the panel condemns it, I should estimate that at least ninety-five percent of the prominent business executives use it without hesitation, along with a similar percentage of professional men, leading politicians, and fashionable hostesses. I should be confident that at least seventy-five percent of the attendants at this conference use it regularly; at least I know that most of my colleagues do. Shall we then be relevant if we teach all our students, including those who have never labored in their minds and never want to, that all people, from presidents of the United States on down, who use *myself* objectively are "prissy idiots"? Even usage, the most widely approved aspect of language study, will be more or less relevant depending upon what we teach and to whom we teach it.

Accordingly, we are entitled to ask ourselves whether or not we have been teaching language, enough of language, and the most important aspects of language. Here we shall encounter wide divergence of opinion and practice. The editors of the dictionary I have been quoting apparently believe we should condemn the objective use of *myself* and perhaps should suggest that it is the prissy practice of idiots. Personally, although I believe I use *me* in such locutions, I should give the usage of *myself* a relatively low priority. Editors of the same dictionary apparently believe in the teaching of etymology; at least they have included an excellent list of Indo-European bases, and here I should agree with them, although I suspect that they and I are in the minority, at least so far as current practice is indicative. On the other hand, most dictionaries do little to remind us, either in their introductions or in their word entries, of the deep and pervading relationships among the human mind, human society, and human language.

In the light of such diversity, and in a brief statement, I can do little more than enunciate my own convictions. Basically, my belief is that language should be taught on the broadest practicable bases and at all levels, and that on the whole we have been too narrow and too limited in our teaching. We have tended to teach the minutiae like spelling and usage—which are of course desirable within limits—but we have mainly neglected teaching language as mind, language as thought, language as the means of society. Of course there are limits to which philosophical concepts can be taught to young minds or to dull adults, but the mathematicians have shown us that even very small children can grasp ideas that trouble their parents. Something of the sort must be true of language; we now know that infants can themselves develop the idea of a symbol, and if they can do this, children can wrestle with ideas much more complex and sophisticated than those that most teachers have been giving them. The difficulty has been that we have not much tried to teach an understanding of the nature of language, partly because many teachers have never asked themselves what language is and how it works, nor have they assumed that asking searching questions about language was any of their business, whether the questions were asked of their students or of themselves.

Along the same lines, I believe we should teach for long-time effects. Learning to use language well is a slow process; language learning begins within the first weeks of a child's life and continues at least until senility; we should be much more concerned with motivating language study, with showing students how to improve their grasp of language through the years and the decades than with making the short-term corrections that are the be-all, and unfortunately the end-all, of much inculcation of the native tongue. Specifically, we should be much more concerned with teaching youngsters to grow an adequate vocabulary, to think constructively about the words they use, than with identifying the so-called parts of speech. We should be more concerned with teaching youngsters to handle strong, complex sentence structures, than with avoiding sentence fragments, more inclined to teach precise and economical subordination than with keeping supposed prepositions away from the ends of sentences.

On the whole, then, I should say that the broader the teaching of language, the more relevant it is likely to be. Of course students may not see this; and as a matter of fact, parents and school boards may not, either, but something can be done about such lacks of understanding if the teacher himself knows enough language to make it significant and exciting. Thus perhaps the best way to make language teaching more relevant is to study more language, for the teacher himself to study language. Naturally, no generalization like that above can be always and equally applicable; pride used to be considered the first of the Seven Deadly Sins, but teaching a ghetto child an honest pride in his native dialect may become highly relevant. Even in such a restricted area, however, the teacher may find he can work best with ghetto dialects if he approaches them in light of the whole problem of dialect, of the nature of language as it expresses itself through dialect. Here, once more, to be relevant, the teacher must understand language. Not all teachers do, at least not well enough to apply the idea that dialects are essential to language, that healthy languages cannot exist without them, and thus dialect is something to be welcomed, not anything to be ashamed of. Furthermore, if a child has learned one dialect, he can certainly learn another one, a standard dialect, if he needs it.

I should say that we have in the past tended to teach grammar too much, and that if we wish to be relevant, we should teach vocabulary and rhetoric more than we have. I believe we should make more use than we have of what we are now discovering about language learning, that specifically we need to make language acquisition more exciting, and that this can be done with such approaches as etymology and semantic change. Lastly, we should re-examine the lesser aspects of language study, the teaching of usage and mechanics, for example, to see how much of each of these may be relevant to the kinds of youngsters that appear in our various sorts of classes. That is, language study is by its nature relevant for the human race, but when we consider what we are to do in our classrooms we must always be concerned with particular aspects of language study, and here we should ask, Relevant for what? Relevant for whom?

-⊰ 5. ⊱-

The Gospel
According to Lindley Murray:
or What Must the Teacher of Grammar
Do to Be Saved?

If this "lecture" seems a bit disjointed, the reason may be that it has been rejointed, put together out of two papers I read during 1956 and 1957, the first to the Nevada Council of Teachers of English, the other to the corresponding organization in Colorado. Both talks were reproduced for the membership of the respective organizations, but have not otherwise been published.

--⟨ There was once a great American Prophet who had come out from the City of Brotherly Love, and his words went trumpeting through the land.

"Repent ye," he said, "and worship grammar, for Bishop Lowth has come to save us from solecisms. The wages of syntax —or anyhow, the wages of the faulty use of syntax—are death."

Forthwith, a book came from his mouth, and flew off in all directions, and wherever Little Red Schoolhouses popped up there popped up also Lindley Murray's Good Book. So orderly it was, and so positively authoritative, that few dared deny the least syllable of its demonic addition. It became Gospel, and by it the inept were damned and the grammatical were saved as prescribed in the Gospel According to Lindley Murray. This went on through many generations of men, and through dozens of profitable editions. English grammar, or what passed for English grammar, became the head of the corner of the American school system, and Murray's priests officiated at a sort of daily sacrament, in which the English language was transmogrified into a hodgepodge of parts of speech.

So, for many decades the voice of the authoritarian grammarian was heard in the land, and this continued until the present century. In fact, it continues today, although falteringly, for lately the conviction has grown that Lindley Murray, however dedicated he may have been, was a false prophet and his book apocryphal. This new revelation came about through the union of two strange bedfellows, two who can seldom agree about anything: the students of language and the educational testers. The students of language provided the theory. They pointed out that the conventionally accepted statement about English grammar had not been drawn from English at all, but from Latin, and that it described English badly because the grammars of the languages are essentially different. Classical Latin grammar relies mainly upon inflection, whereas English grammar relies mainly upon the arrangement of words in the sentence and upon relationship words. But this was theoretical. No doubt few people but scholars would have cared, for scholars can be defined in the popular lexicon as only slightly different from old-fashioned children which were to be seen but not heard. The scholar is to be heard but ignored. Scholars speak, on the whole, on mankind's deaf side. But the educational testers speak where the public needs no hearing aid, and on this occasion they wasted little time talking about eternal truths. They said that grammar as taught in the schools, right or wrong, did little or no good. They asserted that children do not learn to write or speak by learning grammar, and they seemed to have evidence to support what they said.

So now we are in what an older generation would have called a pretty pickle, with our educational system resting on the grammar school, and no grammar we are sure of to teach in it, and no certainty that we ought to be teaching a grammar if we ever get one. How did we squirm ourselves into this predicament? I am not sure we know very certainly. I am not aware that the history of the teaching of grammar has ever been written, although such a study might provide a more useful dissertation than some which have resulted from the compilation of misinformation dredged up by questionaires. Thus I must apologize for the conjectural nature of my explanation. But I trust it is not far wrong, and it is at least intriguing, for it shows the student of words hoist with his own petar, deceived into a blind following of a tradition which was not there, because he had failed to grasp the implication of the words he was using, failed to note that they had shifted under his gaze.

Why was an American school for younger people called a grammar school? The answer is obvious, because schools for pupils of similar ages in England were called grammar schools, and on the whole we borrowed British terms. And since our schools were grammar schools, what should one teach in them, unless grammar? Accordingly, we taught it. It had not always been so. The Pilgrim Fathers provided their young with the *Bay Psalm Book* and a speller, a restraint in which they resembled the friend of Chaucer's Little Clergeon, who asserted in effect, "I study singing; I don't care much about grammar." But by the eighteenth and early nineteenth centuries, when the American school system was taking form, grammar was becoming the fad, and grammar books were available—Noah Webster's *Grammatical Institute* along with the redoubtable Murray—and eventually many others.

Thus we got the name for the grammar school from British education, but what was a British grammar school? The original grammar schools were founded mostly in the sixteenth and seventeenth centuries, and later schools were called grammar schools in imitation of them. They existed to teach "grammar" to the young—but not the grammar of English—and not even to teach exclusively the linguistic structure of any language. The root of the word in Greek, *graphein*, meant *to write*, as in our word *telegraph*, and *gramma* meant anything written. A grammar school existed to study anything written on an elementary level, in the universal language, Latin. True, the grammar schools did not teach grammar in the sense of the nature and use of a language, but only the nature and use of the Latin language. All through the Middle Ages education had rested upon learning Latin, because everything of any consequence was written in Latin and once a man had that language all secrets were unlocked to him. But construing Latin exactly required a knowledge of Latin grammar in the limited sense of parts of speech and cases and inflections with which to identify them, and since Latin grammar was unlike any grammar that an English boy had acquired by learning English naturally, it had to be learned as a subject to be studied formally. The boy who studied Latin grammar in a grammar school did not study English grammar there, or at least not much of it. Certainly he did not study what often passes for grammar in American schools, that barefoot half-sister of grammatical study: the standards of correct usage. He studied grammar because Latin was a foreign language but the foundation of learning, and when he had learned to read Latin he went on studying "grammar," but now "grammar" was the simplified learning of the world, even the writings upon occult and forbidden sciences, as the word *gramary* still attests. A grammar school was a school in which students studied the elements, the elements of anything and everything.

In fact, the evidence suggests that even Roman students did not much study Latin grammar. They did not need to. They would

study Greek grammar to learn Greek, and they gave great attention
to the study of language, but to the study of rhetoric, not of grammar in the restricted sense. Of course the Roman scholars studied
grammar, as the Greek scholars had. It was their business, and they
did it well, as I take it scholars should study grammar always and
everywhere. But the evidence seems to be scanty that Roman teachers thought the young had any business with Latin grammar. The
young did have business with functioning language, with the principles of expression and the means of using them. "Language power
for youth," I imagine we would call it, but their term was *rhetoric*.

So now, although our educational system stems from Classical
culture, we have greatly weakened the study of rhetoric in our
schools and proliferated the study of "grammar," whatever its exponents mean by grammar. How has this change come about?
Where do we get what we teach under the heading of language use?
I am not sure I know, but I am convinced that central in our dealing with the native language are two very strong traditions of what
to do and not to do, and as symbols of these I shall adopt two of
their notable manifestations, Lindley Murray's grammar and the
Little Red Schoolhouse.

The two Americans who have most influenced the growth of
American English are presumably Noah Webster and Lindley Murray. Both were trained as lawyers. Webster's name is known to every
school boy; Murray's is almost forgotten. Webster never managed to
live as a lawyer, starved as a schoolteacher, survived mainly from
the proceeds of his blue-backed speller, and celebrated his three
score and ten by bringing out the volumes through which the pat-
ronym *Webster* became synonymous in American English with
dictionary. Murray, his slightly older contemporary, made a fortune
practicing law in Philadelphia, retired at forty, moved to England,
and being a devout Quaker, apparently expected to devote his life
to writing religious tracts. Incidentally, he prepared a little so-called
grammar (extensively but not exclusively a treatment of usage) for
use in a neighboring Friends' school. He added a reader and speller.
They became popular, "to the exclusion of all others," in both England and America, and by his death when he was eighty-one, had
sold more than a million and a half copies. They represented au-

thority on the language for many millions of children and for the children of these children. Most of the Murray grammars have been worn back into the rag pulp from which they sprang.

I rehearse this bit of biography to suggest how incidental all this was. If Murray felt that in dealing with language he was sowing the seeds of civilization, molding men's minds, refining the tools with which we understand or fail to understand one another, I find little evidence of such awareness inside or outside his writings. He seems to have been mainly concerned that the young avoid mistakes. Even this concern he developed in part because people seemed to want to buy his books. He had the fair-mindedness of a devout Friend and the persuasiveness of a Philadelphia lawyer; he made excellent textbooks, excellent in the sense that they were clear, orderly, and judicial. But what was he teaching, or rather, what was he writing which became the linguistic word of God to thousands of teachers?

He epitomized a tradition. Practically speaking, grammars of English did not exist prior to the eighteenth century, and when they did appear they were an adjunct of the whole eighteenth-century concern for proper conduct. Lord Chesterfield disapproved of the natural expression of human emotions in laughter because it promoted a horrible distortion of the face, and eighteenth-century writers upon language called the natural and native use of the English language blasphemous and barbarous because they felt that usage was a reprehensible distortion of universal grammar. For the measure of universal grammar—however mistakenly—they accepted the grammar of Latin, and this grammar notably as embodied in the tradition that grew from the works of another fortuitous maker of textbooks, the fourth-century Donatus, who had written an elementary work on the supposed eight parts of speech in Latin. Now this book was a bit ridiculous even for Latin and even in its day. Rabelais makes great fun of it, but it spread as Murray spread, presumably because it was simple and orderly, not because it was a profound commentary on the great Latin language, on the nature of all language, or upon the role of language in society.

Thus the discussion of language in the eighteenth century was not so much concerned with understanding language, what it is and how it works, as it was with determining what was right and what was wrong, what was called elegant and refined as against what was called barbarous. When the writers made these decisions they seldom seriously consulted the English language itself; they determined how this locution would appear if it were Latin, and if that did not work, or sometimes even if it did, each writer consulted his own personal whim, declared this whim to be eternal right and all others to be eternal wrong. For instance, James Buchanan, a grammarian of the day, asserted "*It's* for *it is* is vulgar; *'tis* is used." George Harris, asserted that "handleing a subject," "driving a bargain," and "bolstering up an argument," were all "common, but very disgustful!" James Harris, who in *Hermes* often talked eminent good sense when he discussed universal grammar as philosophy, also dealt with usage; he declared that "ADO is an Abbreviation of *to do* [which, of course, it is not] and ought never to be used by any man, who has the least Regard for the English Language or his own credit." There were some dissenting voices. Joseph Priestly, for example, a Unitarian minister with little linguistic training, had an open mind, but his little grammer went almost unnoticed, while the thunderings of Noah Webster in this country, and of Bishop Robert Lowth in Britain drowned him out, until they were all innundated by Lindley Murray's suave imitation in both countries of the redoubtable bishop. Priestly was so much persecuted for his liberalism—albeit more for his political than his grammatical liberalism—that he finally emigrated. In this country his political liberalism was not suspect, and his grammatical liberalism went unnoticed. Meanwhile, Murray's grammars held much of the field until well into the nineteenth century, when they were superseded by volumes with a more familiar style, such as those by Samuel Kirkham, or by those with more ponderous apparatus, pioneered by Goold Brown.

What was Murray's grammar like? You all know, even though you may never have seen a copy. Most of you who teach grammar today could use it and not change your courses much. It might sound a bit quaint, but more in Murray's pseudo-classical sentence structure than in any rules he lays down or the definitions he pronounces. There are minor variations; after the fashion of the day he defined punctuation by the pause in speaking, and recommended counting *one* for a comma, *one one* for a semicolon, *one one one*

for a colon—a mark more used then than now—and *one one one one*
for a period. Essentially, then, Lindley Murray presents the subject
matter that is still being taught in most of the schools in the country. I suspect that if half my freshman class this autumn had been
taught with Lindley Murray, and the other half by modern but conventional grammars, I should not be able to tell the difference in
the products. Now the tragic fact here is not so much that Murray
was wrong; often he was. How could he help it? After all, Latin
grammar is mainly an inflectional grammar and English grammar
is mainly what we call distributive or analytic; the two are basically
different, and to ask an English speaker to learn from a Latin grammar is rather like requiring a surgeon to learn his medicine only
from books on dentistry. The horrible fact is that Murray was inadequate, and those books which have never outgrown Murray are
still inadequate. I doubt that Murray knew what language is; if he
did, he did not put the information in his book. He was talking less
about language than about linguistic etiquette.

Now, there is nothing wrong with teaching what we suppose
to be proper and elegant speech, so long as we do not suppose that
we are teaching language, the whole of language, or even the most
important aspects of language when we do so. Not that Murray
should have been expected to know much about language. He was
a good Quaker, a good lawyer, a good textbook writer, doubtless a
good husband and father, but he never much studied language. If
his book had become no more than he originally intended it, a
simple statement to tell small girls how to speak and write properly,
all would have been well. But it became the standard pronouncement upon language, the pattern to grow minds by.

Lindley Murray's grammar was a good textbook in its day; I
take it also that the dodo was a modern bird in his day and the
surrey with the fringe on top a good means of transportation in
frontier Oklahoma. But any teacher who wants to feel that he is
rising to his high calling of teaching man to use his most useful
tool, had better outgrow Lindley Murray's concept of language as
linguistic etiquette.

So here we are with a tradition of teaching the native grammar to young people. What we have been teaching is not the grammar of any known language, but selected portions of Latin gram-

mar, with adaptations to English, and great gaps where much of the grammar should be, provided we can agree that we ought to teach it. Certainly, teaching it does little harm. I assume, also, that few would deny that it does some good. Almost anything which calls people's attention sharply and repeatedly to language does good. Anagrams do, so does Skip-Across. Teaching children to read sentences backward would help, but it is questionable if any of these devices help enough so that we are entitled to give much school time to them.

What, then, should we do? There are always about three courses: drop the thing, alter the thing, or get something different. Naturally, all three have been suggested.

A good case can be made for dropping the study of grammar as a major subject in the secondary schools. Certainly much that is taught under the heading of grammar is not very important for the prospective plumber or housewife. To understand and be understood one need not be able to distinguish the various uses of *singing* in *singing training, singing cowboy, is singing,* and *start singing.* You and I may not be able to agree on these distinctions, and if we can, the average youngster, or the average man or woman, scarcely needs to be able to make the distinctions and name them. The distinctions among adjectives, verbals, and parts of verbs are extremely difficult, and no one needs to make them in order to compose good prose or to understand it when someone else has composed it. Even the ordinary distinctions, such as those between adjectives and adverbs, are difficult, and perhaps impossible to draw. Presumably a youngster should be able to distinguish between *good* and *well,* between *done* and *did,* and if youngsters do not learn this naturally, as those in literate homes do, they may as well be taught the usage in school. There is at least as much reason to teach them to say, "He invited Mary and me" as there is to teach them how to brush their teeth, to shift gears, or to ride in an airplane. Furthermore, if you can tell the youngster that *me* is the objective form and that in this sentence it is a direct object, he may understand sooner and better. Of course he may not understand at all, but that is another matter. The fact probably is, however, that if the youngster ever learns to say, "He invited Mary and me," he learns the distinction as he learns that between *infer* and *imply,* between *criticism* and *objection,* by imitation and by habit, although of course the teacher can help by telling him and by jogging his memory. That is, most usage in a native tongue is learned naturally, or it is never learned at all.

A young person learns much of his grammar in the same way. Long before he ever goes to school he has learned the essential patterns of the language. He learns very early to ask for an ice cream cone, and to say that he does or does not want his orange juice. He learns to say *two ice cream cones* and not *very ice cream cone* when he wants more than one, and he is quite aware, at least functionally, of the grammatical principles and practices involved. That is, whether we teach them or not, children know most of the grammar and usage they need, and most of them cannot be taught much usage in a classroom anyhow. A few who come to us saying *he don't* can be taught to say *he doesn't,* but most of those who say *he don't* at twelve will say it at fifty, and they will probably move in circles in which their companions say *he don't* and they may as well say it too, and be popular. Some usage we can appropriately teach, and I assume that none of us would settle for less, but if we reduce the teaching of the native tongue to upholding *am I not* and denigrating *ain't I* we have reduced it to very little.

Are we, then, to limit the teaching of English to the teaching of a little usage? I trust not. Before we markedly reduce the teaching of our native tongue, we should remind ourselves that many of the great cultures seem to have founded their educational systems on the close study of language and literature, especially upon the classics in the native language and on the use of language in composition, oral and written. The study of Chinese classics was for centuries the basis of Chinese culture, and of all the great cultures still alive Chinese has been the most durable. Or consider Egyptian education. A bright young Egyptian boy was turned over to a government official. There he observed the construction of buildings, the administration of offices, but he spent much of his time copying letters and then composing letters of his own. He would, for example, copy a letter which might be summarized as follows:

> Don't be a baker's apprentice. He will dangle you by the heels down into the bake oven while you pick up the loaves of hot bread for him. If he happens to drop you, you

will be burned alive. Learn to write excellent letters. Then you can become a government official, have an easy life, and always get good pay.

And how do we know that this happened? Because of what are called *ostraca*, the waste pieces of stone chipped off in building. The ostraca around such edifices as the Pyramids were scratched with students' compositions, which the young Egyptians had written on the only available scrap material, ready for correction by the government official in charge, who had to be a sort of Freshman English teacher as well as a construction engineer. Even after the student had been "graduated" and given an administrative job, he continued to study style, for he could expect advancement when some superior executive was attracted by the purity, the elegance, or the vigor of his letters and reports.

Or consider Rome. An ambitious young Roman studied language, particularly the use of language, oral and written. He even went to Greece to study it, not because he was mainly interested in Greek, and not because he was studying grammar, but because the best teachers of rhetoric were the Greeks. And this veneration for the study of language continued into Christian times. Augustine was a teacher of rhetoric; without this background in language and literature he probably would not have been one of the most influential men in the western world. Similarly, an Italian cardinal discouraged one of his fellows from much reading of the Bible, lest Jerome's indifferent Latin, into which the Holy Word had been translated, corrupt the purity of a good classical style. For centuries the study of language and literature was the basis of English education, and of much European education. And here one might remind oneself that the products of British education spread the language and the influence of a little island (England proper is less than half the size of the state of Nevada) throughout the world. If the products of our classrooms are as well fitted to live in our society as Confucius, Caesar, and Shakespeare were fitted to live in theirs, we shall not have done badly. We can, I believe, slight the study of language and literature only at our peril.

--◄{ 6. }►--

Trouble in
Linguistic Paradise

This lecture was more heterodox when it was first read to the Oregon Council of Teachers of English in 1955 than it is at this writing. The historically minded will recall that Chomsky's basic statement *Syntatic Structures, Janua Linguarum* No. 4 ('S–Gravenhage, 1957) was not published until after the original reading of this lecture, but the word had leaked out through Chomsky's writings in *Language* and his appearances at linguistic meetings. The "Carpenter Fries" mentioned by the Serpent is the late Charles Carpenter Fries whose various writings, by 1955, were bewildering the more complacent teachers of English, especially those who had assumed they were also conversant with grammatical subjects. The lecture was revised for various audiences, and was printed in one version as cited below. I have revised it somewhat to remove ambiguities; specifically I have excised the phrase "Universal Grammar," which I had used with the eighteenth-century connotation of Universal Usage, but the term has since been revived in the more appropriate Cartesian sense; see especially, Noam Chomsky, *Cartesian Linguistics* (New York and London, 1966).

Commitments for the Years Ahead: Proceedings of the [California] *State Conference on English* (1960), pp. 6–16.

---⚜ Once upon a time the User of English dwelt in a paradise known as the Eden of Linguistic Authority, which the Gods of Prescriptive Grammar had made to wall him from the sins of Doubt, Thought, and Unsanctioned Innovation. The plants in the garden were neatly trimmed, freed of all weedy vulgarisms which might suggest the Vulgus, a many-headed beast, who was to be kept out of the garden. Furthermore, the Great I-Decide of Prescriptive Grammar had provided a Rulebook for the Policing of English, and a Usage Ukase Unifier to enforce it, so that there would never be any uncertainty or irregularity about anything, and the garden would retain its beauty and order forever. The Usage Unifier had put labels on the plants identifying them as they had come from the Celestial Inflectional Syntactical Lexicographical Nursery.

There was, for example, the Lexicographical Tree, which bore all the words in the world. True, these words did not grow quite on the tree itself, but they were in the dictionaries, and the dictionaries hung from the boughs of the tree, and in these works the irrefragable facts about the words were culled and recorded, forever to remain unchanged, *saecula saeculorum*. Each of these words the Gods of Prescriptive Grammar had made in their own images, and the user of English could trust the words because once they had been hung from the boughs of the Lexicographical Tree, that was all he knew and all he would ever need to know.

There was also the Trellis of the Authoritarian Decalogue, a rambling vine draped on a series of handsome signs: "Thou shalt not say 'Ain't,'" "Thou shalt not end a sentence with a preposition," "Thou shalt not use the gauche word *get*, which is inelegant," "Thou shalt not say 'It's me,' which is illogical," and many more. By its name the trellis should have had only ten signs, but time out of mind there seemed to have been an infinity of them, and every time the User of English looked at the trellis he noticed some new

35

ones: "Thou shalt not say 'I will' when 'I shall' is correct"; "Thou shalt not confuse *like* and *as* or say 'Everybody took their hats.'"

Then there were the Hedges of Preferred Usage, which were perhaps the most wonderful plants in the garden, for they surrounded everything. True, they seemed to get nowhere but they kept the more circumspect dwellers in the garden from straying into inelegant locutions. They bore few flowers of poetry, and even the fruits of prose might wither on the durable redundancies that proliferated like suckers from the hedges, but they had a consistency that would cry out strumpet-tongued against the deep damnation of their digging up. The User of English was occasionally irked with them since they got in his way, but he hesitated to root any of them out lest he thereby disrupt some ancient symmetry which the Great I-Decide would feel was very real, although not to the vulgar eye.

Now, there were in the Garden creeping and crawling things, which would skitter under the Hedges of Preferred Usage and go where they pleased, or they would stray outside the walls of the Garden and bring back ways of saying things which were not in the dictionaries on the Lexicographical Tree, and what concourse they had with these Lilith-like locutions of dubious virtue, it were perhaps best not to inquire. One of the cleverest of these creatures was a serpent known as the Modern Linguist, a pernicious fellow, always up to mischief. He would entice the Termites of Research to riddle the signs in the Trellis of the Authoritarian Decalogue, and would whisper slyly to the fat, well-dressed words in the dictionaries, "Did you know, my dear, that your occasional linguistic slips are showing?"

Naturally, the conduct of this serpent troubled the User of English, and one day when he caught the reptile slithering out of a sort of den he had concocted out of multigraphed monographs, linguistic institutes, and rejected allophones, the User accosted him, saying "Look here. I want a conference with you."

"You mean you wish to transform a few morphemes?" the serpent asked slyly, knowing full well that the words *phoneme* and *morpheme* always made the User of English blush for shame.

But the User was not abashed. Recalling his course in English Minus 1, The Principles and Practice of Approved Jargon, he said

firmly, "You are featuring a position of maintaining an uncoopera-
tive attitude toward certain aspects of the circumstances involving
conditions not approved in the regulations, and accordingly I am
about to emphasize taking under consideration the expediting of a
report."

During this speech the serpent had had plenty of time to twist
himself up the Tree of the Knowledge of Good and Evil Speech.
"The trouble with you, my friend," he said, "is that you have too
little poetry in your soul. Even a bit of doggerel would do you no
harm. For whatever good it may do, here is a jingle I have been
puttering with." Then he recited as follows:

> Oh, purist with zeal thermostatic,
> Devoted to forms hieratic,
> Degoggle your eyes
> And try on for size,
> Something morphophonematic.

The serpent disappeared among the leaves, but the User of
English could still hear him muttering, as though to himself,

> A pedagogue aptly called Domsky,
> Never got loose from his Momsky,
> He approached his demise
> With Carpenter Fries,
> But wait till he hears about Chomsky!

The User of English was outraged. He assumed that these
limericks were not intended for him, but there was that crack about
the goggles. He was outraged, but he was also intrigued. True, he
was wearing goggles, and the Great I-Decide had strictly forbidden
him to remove them. Still, I-Decide did not come around as often
as he used to, and accordingly the User slipped the goggles side-
ways for just a peep. Then in amazement he took them off and
stared.

The Garden was no longer there. Or it was so changed that
at first it seemed not to be there. He could stroll through the
Hedges of Preferred Usage, which were full of holes. Even the
neat little Parts of Speech were lopping every which way, having

little to stand on. The dictionaries still dangled from the Lexico-graphical Tree, but the definitions in them no longer looked like the codification of eternal truth. And now the User of English was taken with a staggering surmise. Suppose there were no Gods of Prescriptive Grammar, and the Great I-Decide himself a quack or a hoax? Suppose that language had not been made in the images of the Gods of anything, but that he himself, the User of English, had made his language in his own image, not even in his best image, but had blundered into much of it, as it were accidentally, when he was not thinking at all, so that it reflected, along with other things, that little unselfconscious self of dubious repute with Freud-ian overtones—and the Lord knew what undertones—which another serpent, the Modern Psychologist, had been telling him about?

By the time such questions had been asked, the User of English found himself well outside anything which could any longer be called an Eden of Linguistic Authority. Like Milton's Adam and Eve, "some natural tears he shed, but wiped them soon; the world was all before him." If he could discover nowhere the order and symmetry which he had once supposed existed in the garden of his mother tongue, he found that the more human his language ap-peared to be, the more interesting it became. It was a bit like a charming baby, his own offspring, which he could chuck under the chin, while listening to it gurgle. Accordingly, he set to ex-amining it, and in the last half century he has discovered a good bit. Meanwhile, he found that his old enemy, the Modern Linguist, was quite a chummy fellow, and what they found together has con-siderable importance for teachers of English. Let us have a look at some of it.

This linguistic revolution, this new look in language, or what-ever you wish to call the results of recent thinking about our mother tongue, can be summarized under three headings: the word on the word, the new standard for standards, and the grammar of gram-mar. [Perhaps this vista of the new look can be omitted; it will be sketched from more recent points of view in the lectures below.]

—◄ 7. ►—

New Thoughts
on the Same Old Language

This lecture was prepared to accommodate an emergency when a scheduled speaker at the general session of the National Council of Teachers of English, meeting in Denver in 1959, was called abroad. Under the circumstances, I felt privileged to pillage a book I had written but not yet published, *Thinking about Language* (New York, 1959), even as to phraseology, which I did with the kind permission of the publishers, now Holt, Rinehart & Winston.

Ball State Teachers College Forum, I (1960), 17–28.

Recent decades have seen one revolution after another in language, in our thinking about it, in our learning to work with it, in the tools we now have for teaching it. These revolutions are more pervasive than they may have seemed to us as we lived through them and absorbed them with our morning grapefruit and our afternoon relief that the last class was over. At least they are more inclusive than I had recognized them to be until I deliberately counted one by one my blessings, or my bludgeonings, as you elect to term them. Perhaps I may count them over with you, and in doing so I shall unblushingly lean upon a little book I recently prepared for the Rinehart pamphlet series called *Thinking About Language*—I mention this so that if you ever encounter this work you will know that any similarity between the two is not coincidental at all. It is just plain cribbing and destitution of mind —on the analogy of *suicide*, what you might call, *suiplagiarism.*

The first revolution occurred in etymology, in our notion of where language came from, and what has happened to languages after they got started. In a way, we have all absorbed this knowledge; I find that most modern teachers are surprised to learn that as late as two centuries ago scholars argued not as to whether God gave man language as a single act, but whether he bestowed the gift on the plains of Chaldea or somewhere in the Holy Land. Although teachers know the story of the Tower of Babel and how the Lord confounded the languages of the builders, they assume that this picture of the builders vanishing in all directions and taking their confounded languages with them, is only a sort of handsome trope reflecting language dispersal, and need not be interpreted literally. Modern teachers know that however languages got that way, they appear to us in great language families, that English is one of the members of the most influential of all these groups of language, the Indo-European. They know that whether language arose from imitating *bow-wow's,* or *pooh-pooh's,* or *boo-hoo's,* or whether language came not from imitation but almost spontaneously from man's longing and grew because he had memory and attention span, a knowledge of how language has grown promotes an understanding of it, and even helps students to learn it.

Here is a great body of exciting knowledge, knowledge that can have all the enchantment of a game for young learners, how words descend from earlier words, shifting in form and meaning, scintillating in the amazing phantasmagoria that is the history of language, a tale that has the magic of a fairy story and the sweep of time and the depth of human kind. Are we using these power-ful and fascinating tools that have been put into our hands? To a degree we are, and apparently more and more. When I was an undergraduate I was told that I would do well to study Latin because English had borrowed from it. That was good advice so far as it went, but nobody suggested to me that I ought to study the growth of the English language, too, because our minds and our cultural beings are enshrined in it, or that studying language as civilization's essential tool was any of my business.

This is changing; I take it that any college department of English that does not these days suggest something of the sort to its students is an outdated department. More courses are being taught in vocabuary, and more of them now make use of etymol-ogy; these courses have become something more than juggling prefixes and suffixes, although that legerdemain can have its use. English courses in the secondary schools and freshman English courses in college are making more of language as language, but few of them as yet make much of the materials from etymology. For instance, I know not one popular textbook that has in it even a brief list of Indo-European bases, and I should doubt, on the basis of my personal acquaintance, that there are in the room a half dozen people who could give me on demand a half dozen bases in Indo-European. I believe we should all be able to do at least this; we should find our teaching more fun and our students would find us more exciting if we could. I would doubt, also, that there are many people in the room who have voluntarily gone to the dictionaries and have worked out the history and growth of one single word from Indo-European to modern English, but we would all be better teachers if we would do so. If we are to make the teaching of English a personal affair we must make the English language a personal experience, and a nodding acquaintance with its progenitors is a natural part of the experience, a sort of linguistic PTA meeting, in which we come to know the children through the parents. [Subsequently, brief lists of Indo-European bases appeared in a few textbooks, and at this writing there is an excellent one in the *American Heritage Dictionary*.]

This revolution, the upsetting of our notions as to where language came from and how it has grown, is pretty well complete, but some revolutions in language are yet violently in progress. Among these is the explosion in our notions of the nature of meaning. This all started with two English professors, as much as with anybody—English both in their profession and their birth, I. A. Richards and C. K. Ogden. Like many of us, they were born into a world which supposed that words have meaning, but they changed all that. They saw that words have referents and that they serve as symbols to call up meaning, that the meaning, whatever it is, remains in us, not in the word. This revolution has been well publicized, partly through the activities of the general semanticists, and accordingly, I shall do little to describe it, but just to be sure we are standing on common ground here, I might offer an example. Suppose I pronounce the syllables, *Nick Hook*. These words have a referent, the executive secretary of this organization; we all agree as to who the referent of these words is, but we do not know, just from the words, what he is. They do not tell us whether he helps doddering elderly ladies across muddy streets or purloins lollypops from squalling children. The words have a referent, but little meaning. If now I change the use of these words, and say, "What the NCTE needs is just one more Nick Hook as executive secretary," the words stimulate a sense of meaning, although different meanings for each of us. For instance, it is conceivable that somebody in the room thinks that Nick has been a bad secretary, that the NCTE is a nefarious organization, that one more bad secretary would wreck it completely, and that this is a consummation devoutly to be desired. This is certainly not what I would mean by the words; I trust I need not say that I should mean quite the opposite, but my point is that the meaning is in me and you and everybody, not in the words themselves. We are the reservoirs of meaning, and the word is a sort of dipper with which we dip up meaning, but when we dip we dip into ourselves, each man getting his own dipperful which is different from all other dipperfuls, even though the word and the referent remain constant.

Of course, practically, words have a sort of meaning, at least if you define *meaning* as an approximation of what a word can be expected to call up in the bulk of the users of the language. Language works by our agreements rather than our disagreements about it; our experience with words is so vast, and we have done so much—most of it unconscious—to order and generalize this experience, that we can use words as though we all agree as to what they mean and what they are good for. On that ill-founded though useful assumption mankind makes laws, and enforces them, builds houses and sells them, proposes marriage, and discusses God. We live by a world of meaning which has no real foundation outside ourselves.

Thus we communicate by the overlapping areas of our meanings, but we do not always rely only on the overlappings. Words can cause fights as well as friendships. Suppose I say, "Professor Snicklepoof? Oh, yes, quite a radical thinker." By this I may mean to compliment the professor by suggesting that the quality of his mind recalls the etymology of the word, Latin *radix*, root. He goes to the roots of things. Or I may mean, presumably *because* Professor Snicklepoof goes to the roots of things, that he is startlingly original and thus evolves ideas other thinkers would miss. If I use the phrase "radical thinker" only in the presence of those who will understand my implications, all may be well. But to some people *radical* can imply no good. To them it suggests a dangerous person, different from the norm in a subversive way, and probably unpatriotic, blasphemous, and immoral.

This uncertainty of meaning can lead to private differences or international disaster. Most such misunderstandings are unintentional, but the ambiguous use of words can be deliberate. Poets get some of their best effects by studied ambiguity. Andrew Marvell wrote,

The grave's a fine and private place,
But none, I think, do there embrace.

Here *private* has overtones. Certainly the grave is private; the occupant is alone with the worms. Not a secluded canoe in the shade of the willows, not a parked car on a lonely road, not a dim-lit sofa after the parents have gone to bed can supply such privacy as does the grave, and Marvell suggests that no one puts his grave to such uses as privacy sometimes promotes. This studied ambiguity of language is providing us with a whole new school of subtle poets and a school of even more subtle, not to say double-talking diplomats, but the question remains: How do words "mean"?

We have had theories, of late, and I shall mention two, partly because they may seem to be as contradictory as possible, and partly because they may yet prove to be complementary. The first is that of binary choices, a theory which stems from specialists who are not students of language at all in the sense that philologists are students of language, from neurologists and communications engineers. This theory rests upon a new notion of mind, that neurons are electrical conductors which can make yes-or-no decisions and that these decisions can grow from the apparently satisfactory or unsatisfactory results of previous yes-or-no decisions. To see how this theory works, let us consider the traditional problem of the child touching a hot stove. The neurons report pain; to us there seem to be various possible solutions, to draw back the finger, smash the stove, amputate the offending digit, endure the pain on the theory it will not go on burning forever, and the like, but to the individual neurons involved no such varied possibilities present themselves. Each of the neurons has only a binary choice, move or do not move, and drawing the finger from the stove results from a very large number of move-decisions. Thus the reaction to pain becomes a series of decisions, jump or don't jump, squall or don't squall, with all the multiple yes-decisions which go into jumping and squalling. If jumping and squalling seem to have a good record in emergencies, the child learns to jump and squall. These reactions are of course relatively simple, but presumably all actions are the results of almost numberless choices, and the difference between drawing a finger back from a hot stove and composing a symphony reflects the number not the nature of the binary choices. Knowledge and use of language, also, grow from binary choices, so that the child learns to say "some candy" and not "candy some" because he always encounters the sounds in one sequence and not in the other; "some candy" occasions yes-choices and "candy some" no-choices. That is, the meaning of *some* is a multiple of its experienced occurrence; a word, like a young lady, is known by the company she keeps, and a definition is only a coded statement of the word's privileges of occurrence in connection with other words. To most of us this seems like a clumsy concept of definition, not very likely to be useful in teaching Johnny to read. The mind boggles at the thought of the number of binary choices that must lie behind every use of every word, and we can scarcely conceive that even an electric brain could make so many choices instantaneously. Of course the communications engineer can retort that our brains are electric, and that whether or not we can comprehend this working of the brain it is the way the brain works and we had better take it into account, that although this may seem a clumsy definition of definition it is the only accurate one, brains being what they are. Accordingly, communications engineers are even now counting the occurrences of words in their circumstances, and using computers to do the reckoning, hoping thus to obtain an accurate and objective statement of definition and meaning.

Now let us turn to the second modern approach to meaning, which stems from symbols and man's sense for them. That man is a symbol-loving creature and that all words are symbols, is no news. We readily make symbols. For example, take two parallel slanting lines; for most people they do not mean much, but revolve one of them so that it bisects the other and you have a letter of the alphabet and the *x* that marks the spot; revolve them a bit and elongate one and you have the cross associated with ecclesiastical architecture, with Christ, Christianity, salvation, and a whole host of religious concepts. Thus, crossed lines can become symbols, but we are now coming to realize that man is not the only lover of them, that all the higher animals use symbols, and that the sense for symbol may lie back of language and thus be even more important in the origin and growth of tongues than we had supposed. A whistle may become a sign to a dog, and a trained sheep dog may learn a whole sequence of whistles that become a sort of simple language. Perhaps man is civilized because he was a lover of symbols and became capable of building them in quantity and variety. Certainly language must have been born when a sound became a symbol, when a cry of fear became a warning of the source of the fear, or a sigh of delight meant "I love you."

Furthermore, man craves order. Living in a confused and frightening world he hopes that order will promote his understanding and perhaps lessen his fear. A passion for order promotes the search for God, the belief in science, the devotion to art, the need for philosophy, the love of mankind, which are all in varying degrees answers to the need for order, intellectual and emotional. Meaning is our means of conscious order, and words—or symbols if you wish to call them that—are the means of ordering meaning. Man finds order by generalizing, and he embodies his generalization in words.

Are words, then, only the nuclei for symbol-clusters, and meaning only man's answer to his need for order, an order he finds through symbol? This is at least a pleasant way to think of vocabulary, but it has the limitations notable in some other observations about meaning, that it is neither detailed nor specific. We may yet have to rely on the binary choices of neurons, the choices counted by an electric calculator, to know anything specific about meaning. On the other hand, the two approaches are not incompatible. Symbol may show us why we have words and the electric brain may show us how we have them.

Now to a third revolution; its conclusion is that language is always changing and as a working tool it is made by the users of the language. This may not seem to you revolutionary, but I have only to remind you that less than two centuries ago a great philosopher like Voltaire was writing, "All languages being imperfect, it does not follow that one should change them. One must adhere absolutely to the manner in which the good authors have spoken them; and when one has a sufficient number of approved authors, a language is fixed." This solemn pronouncement now seems to us arrant nonsense; so far as we know, no language is fixed, has ever been fixed, or is ever likely to become fixed. Perhaps nothing else do we know about language in such certainty and detail as that all languages have always changed, and nothing else about languages can be predicted with such confidence as that they will continue to change. A language changes, further-more, in the way the users of the language want it to change, even though this wanting is usually and mainly unconscious. Whatever the users of a language want it to be, provided enough of them want it that way long enough, that it will become. It changes by what we might punningly call "constitutional law"—that is, in accordance with the constitutions of its speakers. Teachers and preachers and editors and parents may promote this change or they may retard it, but they cannot stop it, and sooner or later the users of the language, especially the speakers of the language, will make it into what they want it to be.

This principle has corollaries. One is that no piece of lan-guage, be it a word or a pronunciation or a way of saying things, is essentially any better than any other way. Nothing in language is essentially vulgar or genteel, barbarous or elegant, right or wrong, except as the users of the language want to feel that the locutions have these qualities.

Does this mean, then, that there are no standards at all, no correct and incorrect, no good or bad, no better or worse, no precise or slovenly, no terse or verbose? Some panicky people leaped to this conclusion, but I should say they are leaping with-out looking. One of the papers tomorrow will raise the question, Dare we have standards? I am not on the panel, but if I were I should assert confidently that we do dare have standards, and that if we face the challenge of the day, if we ask ourselves what lan-guage is and how it becomes what it is we can only conclude that we must have standards. After all, who makes the language? You and I and everybody make the language. And what does this hydra-headed language-manufacturer want in his product? Obvi-ously, he wants a number of things; he wants flexibility and versa-tility, but he also wants standards. He may not know just what standards he wants, nor how rigidly he wants them applied, but he does want them in spelling, in punctuation, in diction, in usage, in all aspects of language, and on the whole he relies on people of our sort to inform him which are the best standards and what he should do about them. We had better be prepared to tell him, and to know what we are talking about when we do so.

Like the other revolutions, this one has provided us with marvelous new tools. The most obvious are the new dictionaries, founded upon the historical principles of the philologists and ripened with the study of usage by the modern linguist. But these are improvements upon tools with which we are already familiar; some tools are new, and of them I wish to mention one: linguistic geography. This subject is so new that when a graduate student appeared on our campus asking to work in linguistic geography she was directed to the Department of Geology and Geography in the School of Mines, from whence I had eventually to rescue her.

Linguistic geography is a language technique developed in continental Europe and now being pursued with uncommon vigor in the United States. By means of carefully taken linguistic samples, the scholar is able to identify the forms of a language in time and place, to chart the rise, decline, and movement of these forms, and thus to write the history of language movement upon the face of the earth and to describe with hitherto unknown accuracy the state of any given language today. In Europe the technique has been used to reveal previously unsuspected relationships within the Indo-European language family; here it is employed to describe usage with an accuracy and with an abundance of detail that have never been possible before; at last we are finding out what American English is like and are being presented the details with which to describe and recommend standards with a basis for confidence that no people has previously enjoyed.

Other revolutions there are, aplenty, for instance in our concept of sound, which we now recognize from at least one point of view as the basis of language, but I shall consider tonight only one more revolution, that in grammar. Here we have had a series of *coups d' etat* that would shame a Caribbean dictatorship, and grammatical ideologies have come tumbling in showers upon the graves of already defunct ideologies. Furthermore, the fighting goes on, and nothing suggesting an end is in sight. Some of the history of these revolutions most of you will know, or have at least heard rumored. Two or three hundred years ago, mainly in the eighteenth century, British and American thinkers about language crystallized and popularized what they supposed to be the grammar of English. They were, on the whole, believers in what they called Universal Grammar; that is, they believed that grammar was something like life; there was only one of it and you either had it, more or less of it, or you did not. Presumably the Lord had breathed the breath of life into Adam, and he had likewise breathed the breath of grammar into language. It was all one thing, very much as life is all one thing, and a language had it, more or less of it, or it didn't. Naturally, the students, since they were mainly students of the classics who knew but little Anglo-Saxon and assumed it was a barbarous sort of speech, based their grammars of English upon the grammars of Latin. The reasoning was something like this: grammar is universal; since it is universal the great languages like Latin and Greek will include most of it; the grammar of English would therefore be made up of whatever Latin and Greek grammar could be used to describe English. The grammarians concocted a grammar which was not the grammar of any known language, certainly not the grammar of English, but it was taught in the schools, and the remnants of it are still being taught.

Nor was that all. Within limits, universal grammar must be a reality. Grammar reflects the human mind, and we must assume that all minds have something in common, but this universal quality must be very deep in languages. On the surface, as most users of a language are aware of it, grammar is certainly not universal. Superficially, no two grammars are alike. Furthermore, many of the exponents of universal grammar have been led astray by the same sliding middle term that has misled many purists today. They used the word *grammar* to mean both the way the language works and the correctness or incorrectness of any given locution. That is, they said that a given form in English was barbarous because the same usage did not occur in Latin, and hence it could not be part of universal grammar. In such conduct they were not dealing with grammar at all in any sense that it can be universal, but only with usage, and whatever universal grammar there may be, there certainly is no universal usage. Usage is always local and temporary; it is valid for only one language, often for only certain dialects of a language, and sooner or later it must change. There is nothing universal about usage, or ever can be, but this confusion between a universal grammar, which within limits must exist, and the erroneous concept of universal usage, which cannot possibly exist, led to much confusion in the eighteenth century and is still with us.

During the nineteenth century the philologists took over. They did know Anglo-Saxon, along with other Germanic languages, and they were beginning to make use of what the ethnologists were discovering about primitive languages. They suspected that there was no such thing as Universal Grammar in the old sense, and they understood that Latin and Greek, although they were excellent languages which happened to be the media for great cultures, were still only two languages, essentially no better and no worse than many others, and were certainly without authority to determine what English grammar might be. The grammar of a language, the philologists saw, had to be derived from the language itself—as Latin grammar was derived from Latin—and they accordingly tried to derive English grammar from English. In this they were only moderately successful, for they were mainly students of the classics first and students of language second, and they missed a good bit that is surely English grammar. To offer a facetious example, consider the following: *Preparing the dinner, the host turned on the barbecue spit.* Now the conventional description of a sentence like this is that *on the spit* is a phrase telling where the host is revolving, but unless we assume that *on* is no preposition at all, but part of the verb *turn on,* the guests may be presented with the grisly problem of distinguishing the host from the roast. If this example is more amusing than significant, the manner in which great grammarians like Curme snubbed order in the English sentence is not at all amusing. The result was that not until our day have we had a fresh new look at grammar in modern linguistic studies.

[At this point the original included a survey of various grammatical statements, which is here excised in favors of treatments in the immediately subsequent lectures.]

And now, but a brief word, and I am done. Reviewing, recently, a book on books that had changed the course of history, I observed that a remarkable number of the volumes had stemmed from professors or teachers, or from people who in our society would have been professors or teachers. Inevitably, ours is not the profession which, at any one time, looms most portentous before our fellowmen, but I was constrained to notice, scanning these books, that in the end the head that rules the classroom rocks the world. Very powerful indeed, in this ruling and rocking of worlds, is language, and as we become more aware of the power and the use of language we are rising to that challenge which is our concern this evening. And it seems to me that we are becoming more aware of that challenge, and of what to do about it. More and more we are seeing that life and language are inextricable, and that they are our concern. For life as anything more than the reflexive functioning of the organism requires language. Whatever makes man human rather than bestial may always be inexplicable to man himself, but many a thinker who has started with philosophy or science has had to pass through language and art before he could come back to man and his nature and his ways. It is as though the central mystery of mysteries, the holy of holies of man's nature, were here where the binary choice is becoming mind, where human electrical energy transformed through language becomes functioning. The child's *I want* and *I don't want* become the binomial theorem and concepts of God, but they become through language. Given the power to decide *yes* or *no* and the power to build symbols, all else became possible.

If all this is true, then language forms at the heart, not only of society, but of man himself. Man had an opposable thumb and language, and with them he became civilized. As Vendryes put it, he became *Homo sapiens,* man knowing, because he was *homo loquens,* man talking. If this seems a bit vague, one can only say that most good questions and their answers have always been vague, or erroneous, or both, but that if we can learn what language is and what it can do for man we shall be facing any challenge that our times can offer us.

—◆ 8. ◆—

Grammar:
A Word to Conjure With

This lecture was written at the invitation of Creighton University for an NDEA institute concerned with the present, past, and future of language studies; it was read in Omaha, June, 1968. I gave Creighton permission to publish the lecture in connection with their proposed transactions of the institute, but it has not otherwise been offered for publication. In response to requests, I have somewhat expanded the treatments of tagmemics and stratification.

–⚓ Someday, I hope, someone will write a book that might be entitled, *Words to Conjure With,* treating terms deeply endowed with magical powers. In *Henry IV, Part 1,* Shakespeare makes Glendower boast,

> I can call spirits from the vasty deep,

and Hotspur tauntingly answers,

> Why, so can I, or so can any man;
> But will they come when you do call for them?

Hotspur may have had reason for his skepticism, but something approaching Glendower's supposed power is part of what it means to be human, that he or any man has, with words, the power to call up marvelous things from within the vasty deeps of ourselves. With most words, men can conjure little; few people are wafted into reverie by terms like *of* or *interpenetrability,* but using certain words any man can conjure imperiously. Concepts called up by *mother, faith,* and *Old Glory,* move minds and stir emotions; mainly these words spring from experience, from the past of individuals and the trials of the race, and they seemingly gain their magical powers from human feelings. Thus we may well be surprised to find so intellectual a term as *grammar* among the words to conjure with.

It has long been such a word, albeit sometimes through confusion or misunderstanding. In this country, one cannot attack grammar, as he cannot attack faith or motherhood. He can attack theories or practices of grammar, as one can question theories in theology, but grammar itself, if not quite divine, is still supermundane. And even the attacks upon grammatical approaches evi-

53

dence the power of the word; grammar is one of those subjects that men can fight and curse about. Some of this reverence, I fear, is unwarranted. Frequently, I have asked students if they know why they have not learned to write and speak well; most of them think they know why, and many of them solemnly identify the reason as ignorance of grammar. In almost every instance, I believe, these young people have misdiagnosed themselves. They cannot write because they have not learned to think, or because their habits or their surroundings have not much encouraged a command of vocabulary and rhetoric, or for any of a number of other reasons, but their difficulties do not stem mainly from what either they or I would call grammar.

And this leads us to what grammar is, to what we mean by the word today and what I mean by it tonight. I suspect that my young friends, when they expressed their faith in the curative powers of grammar, were thinking in part of what students of language are more likely to call usage, the etiquette of language. Doubtless my young writers were also expressing their conviction that if a person can identify the so-called parts of speech, if he can infallibly label the adverbs and the adjectives, he will acquire a skill which will mysteriously and almost mystically improve composition. That is, for these youngsters, grammar was whatever was in the grammar book. This definition is similar to, but somewhat different from the use now current among students of language, who would say that grammar is a property of language, the way language works. Any particular language will have its own grammar, the way that language is working at the moment under discussion. Presumably such a grammar can be at least roughly described, and an attempted description of this sort I shall call a grammatical statement.

Before we consider particular grammatical statements, however, we might first consider grammar itself, grammar as a property of language, a property of all languages. Here we might notice that all languages of which we have any knowledge—and they number into the thousands, depending on your definition of language—are made up of two sorts of things. They all contain linguistic units, which from one point of view are sounds or groups of sounds, and whatever else these units may do, many of them are involved in meaning. Speaking very roughly, these units constitute what we call vocabulary, and in English they notably include words. In addition, all languages have some devices for using these linguistic units so that they mean more than they would otherwise, so that they have impacts they could not otherwise command, and they work with an economy that would be impossible without such devices. This is what we call grammar, the way the users of the language handle the linguistic units, so that a combination like, *Presumably all students learn something,* has meaning and impact that these words cannot command when used alone, that they can command only in context.

Granted, then, that language includes meaningful units, you can do either of two things with them, you can put them together or you can keep them apart, and this basic alternative provides us with the fundamental distinction by which we can classify grammar. If you put the units together, you can, of course, put them together in various ways. For example, consider a headline in a recent paper, BACKLASH TO SIT-IN GROWS. *Grows* is the verb and the remainder is the subject, which is made up of *back,* usually a modifier, *lash,* frequently a verb, *to,* presumably a preposition, *sit,* normally a verb, and *in,* normally a preposition, a verbal particle, or an adverb. The whole must be the equivalent of a noun; words that could not usually function as a subject have been made to do so by sticking them together. Likewise, if you add to a word the letter *s,* with or without apostrophe, or the sound/z/, you can make the word work differently. If you add *s* to a word like *beautiful* you destroy the word; it means nothing and you can no longer use it. If you add it to a word like *boy* you augment one of these objects into two or more or you imply some kind of close relationship, as in *the boys' bicycles.* If you add it to a word like *ride* you imply that an action takes place in the singular third person. Now this letter *s* or the sound /z/ has no meaning at all, as do words like *back, lash, sit,* and *in,* but presumably it is the remnant of something which once did have meaning, which has been used so long and so generally that it has become a sort of marker, a signal that can stand as a classifier. As many of you will know, this process, using physical form to suggest grammatical use, is what we call inflection, a device characteristic of many languages that rely heavily upon putting linguistic units together.

Similarly, if you keep linguistic units apart, you can segregate them in various ways and for various purposes. The most obvious is that you can leave them in a string, but change their order. Nor is order the only device you can use if you keep linguistic units apart. Consider the word *of*. Etymologically, this is the same word as *off*, and it formerly had a meaning, something like *away*, as *off* still does in the sentence, *They could not keep the hippies off the street*. In *dozens of copies of the New York Times*, however, *of* has almost no meaning, but shows how the meaningful words in the sentence work together, whereas in the sentence *He is the best man I know of* the word *of* is determining the use of the verb.

Grammatical devices, then, are of two sorts, technically called *synthesis*, putting linguistic units together, and *analysis*, keeping them apart, although—and inevitably in anything as complex as language—the putting together and the keeping apart has become complicated. All languages, apparently, use more than one sort of grammatical device, but most languages use some few quite extensively, and at the expense of most of the others. Indo-European, for example, the ancient ancestor of English and many other languages, made little use of analytic devices, and was so heavily synthetic that it employed hundreds of inflectional endings in many systems, along with incorporation of the subject within the verb and other devices like prefixes, suffixes, and infixes. Modern Chinese, on the other hand, is said to be so heavily analytic that it is almost innocent of inflected forms.

So much for essential processes in grammar. Now that I have finished with them for this evening, I can confess to you that I had an ulterior purpose. I was asked to discuss "Grammar:— Past, Present, Future," and I have no intention of ignoring these instructions. First, then, to the past. I can now survey the history of English grammar in one succinct sentence: In five thousand years or so, English grammar has moved from synthesis toward analysis. In fact, this movement has gone so far that, as some of you will have observed, in giving you the one example of what the spelling *s* or the sound /z/ can do as an ending in English, I almost exhausted the modern English inflectional system. Of all the complex Indo-European verb paradigm, with a dozen or so classes of verbs, each replete with sub-classes revealing tense, mode, and the like, very little is left in English; of the elaborate declension of the noun, which is supposed to have flourished in more than fifteen classes, each with a dozen or so cases and plentiful exceptions, almost nothing survives; the three systems for conjugating the adjective have vanished without a trace. Thus most of the superficial evidence of Indo-European inflection has been lost from English, although, significantly, some characteristics remain. Indo-European had sentences with subjects, and so does English, although some languages emphasize structures which we would not recognize as sentences, or construct sentences centered upon the object. The Indo-European verb system relied in part upon time, and so does the modern English verb, although many grammars do not, at least to the extent that time permeates the verb systems that have descended from Indo-European. Similarly, number has survived in the noun, but the total of ancient survivals into modern English is small.

Most of the grammar of the ancestor of English has been lost. Does this mean we have no grammar? Obviously not. I am speaking, and you are probably understanding most of what I mean to say. We must have grammar, or that would not be possible. If you and I had no more grammar than the rag-tags that have survived from Indo-European, we should be reduced tonight to employing extra-sensory perception. Modern American culture is much more elaborate and complex than Indo-European culture can possibly have been. Modern English must deal with ideas, must provide the basis for social and technological complexity, for which the speakers of Indo-European had neither knowledge nor use. Furthermore, English is so rich in means and devices that it has always supplied users of the language, even the more demanding users, with more linguistic wealth than they could utilize. Inevitably, modern English must embody more grammar than did Indo-European, and as a corollary we must conclude that users of English have been devising grammar faster than they have been abandoning it.

Thus far this evening, I have spoken with a good bit of confidence, but now I must start confessing my ignorance. For example, why has all this come about? We do not know. How is it possible that hundreds of millions of users of the language, speaking on various islands and continents and over thousands of years, have so employed the language that its grammar shifted with some consistency from one kind of basic structure to another? The mind boggles, and we can say only that although we now believe we understand some things about language, much of it remains obscure. Among these obscurities is the next question we should propound tonight: What is the nature of modern English grammar? What is the "present" in that trinity "Past, Present, Future"?

In general we know, but in particular we do not. Obviously, English has developed a relatively rigid word order; words like *the* and *an* always precede the noun and never follow it, and once a word like *the* has been used a sequence has been started that must lead inevitably to some nominal locution. Similarly, we have reworked meaningful words that were not mainly verbs into new words that can combine into complex verb strings, so that although we have lost most of the complex Indo-European verb system based upon conjugation we have developed what is probably an even more elaborate verb system based upon analysis, a system whose beauty we may admire but whose functioning we do not very clearly understand. We have been developing a flexibility in the relationships between the verb and the complement which is so subtle that the grammarian may find himself uncertain as to where the verb ends and the complement begins. All this, however, becomes too multitudinous and too arcane for a popular lecture, and in any event, such details as are pertinent are better treated under the general heading of modern grammatical statements, to which I shall turn shortly. But first a word about the third member of our trinity, the future.

The future, like the past, can be surveyed in one brief sentence: In the near future, English grammar will not change much; over a longer period it is likely to become more analytic. For these conclusions we must rely upon general principles; for the past we rely upon observations, but for the future, those of us who are restricted to mundane knowledge can do no more than extrapolate from the past. In considering the probable future of English grammar, the following three principles are likely to be the most useful: 1) grammar is always changing, but it changes relatively slowly; 2) in language, the broader and deeper the pattern of change, the longer it is likely to operate; and 3) the longer a change operates, the slower it is to stop.

We might discuss these a bit. As for the first, one can observe that no modern language has preserved Indo-European grammar intact, but that grammatical changes are mainly so slow as to be imperceptible. Although English and some other languages have shifted so much in a couple of millennia that the grammar has moved from one major sort to another major sort, apparently nobody noticed any such change, not until hundreds of years after the most dramatic developments. For example, if you could witness one of Shakespeare's plays in his own time, you would probably have difficulty understanding it, partly because the sounds of the language have changed so much in four hundred years that you would have to guess at many of the words. And the words themselves have changed meanings. When Shakespeare makes Hamlet say "Oh worthy pioneer!" you would probably envisage an unkempt fellow jolting around on the seat of a covered wagon or a scientist planning a voyage into space, but to Shakespeare a pioneer was a man who dug tunnels. If, however, you could master the pronunciation and the vocabulary, you would have little difficulty; true, the grammar might seem to you pleasantly quaint at times, but it would not much impede your understanding. To put all this another way, vocabulary, or at least parts of it, can change very rapidly, and our vocabulary has been changing and is continuing to change with remarkable rapidity. Sound can change, rather slowly but very broadly and thus quite perceptibly. Chaucer, for example, noticed sound changes and vocabulary changes in his day, but did not notice grammatical change. Even usage changes, at least particular usages. I was taught not to confuse *provided* and *providing*, although today almost everybody uses them indiscriminately; I was taught that the past participle, preceded by the verb *to be*, should be protected by an insulating *much*. On no condition was one to say, "I am very pleased," although now almost everybody does. Thus grammar in the sense of usage changes, sporadically, sometimes rapidly, sometimes not at all. In the future, even in the near future, we shall have some changes in usage, although just which usages may be hard to predict; we may say with confidence that they will be fought over and they will be few. Changes in grammar, however, will be broad; they will be slow, they will be inevitable, and they will be mainly undetectable in my time, even in yours. Movements in grammar are glacier-like, imperceptible, and mainly irresistible.

Movements in grammar are glacier-like, also, in that they start and stop slowly. The loss of inflection, for example, must have been slow in the millennium before Old English; some consolidation of inflectional systems there had been, but the endings themselves were enduring. In recent centuries, also, the losses have been few, although the process seems to be continuing, but during the Middle Ages endings decayed rapidly. Now the loss of inflection can be considered a broad movement, but it is nowhere near so broad as the whole movement from a grammar mainly synthetic to one mainly analytic. As we have seen, the shift from inflection was only part of the history of the change in English grammar, and if the most obvious movement, it probably was not the most important one or even the controlling one. Inflections seem to have declined because they were no longer needed, because analytic processes had already grown that rendered them obsolete, and some of these analytic growths appear to be thriving in our time. For example, consider the growth of separable verb suffixes, words like *up, in, out, by,* and *over,* when they become parts of verbs. If I say, "My ex-wife turned up at the party," I do not mean to imply that the lady stood on her head, but only that she arrived somewhat unexpectedly. Such structures occur sparsely in Middle English and become fairly frequent in some Renaissance speech. For the last two or three hundred years we have been making them more rapidly than ever before, and this manufacture seems not to be declining in our time. That is, so far as the production of separable suffixes in verbs is concerned, we seem to be fairly high in a long bell curve. We need not assume that the curve will suddenly break off. Nor is the verbal suffix the only evidence of continuing analytic development. The predicate is apparently becoming more fluid, and we are still making new auxiliaries. That is, the evidence seems to be that

English is still moving toward analysis, and particularly since this drift has been in process for some thousands of years, we should not expect it to stop soon. It may change its character; some changes may speed up and others slow down, or they may all decline at different rates, but we can scarcely predict that they will stop, not at least for some time.

We should turn now from what I have called grammar to what I have called grammatical statements, to the attempts to describe grammar. Here again, superficially, we observe great complexity, not to say acrimonious conflict. First, however, let us seek simplicity, and if we do so we shall observe that anyone who endeavors to describe a language needs two things: a body of material to work with and a means of working. Once again, this distinction will permit us to classify, and perhaps better to understand all modern grammatical statements. As for materials to be studied, there are mainly two sorts—it is amazing how frequently linguistic phenomena come in pairs—language already in existence and preserved in some unalterable form, or language latent in individuals, potential, kinetic, capable of becoming active. Of the first sort of language there are again two sorts, language preserved in writing through such media as script and printing, and oral language preserved by transcription or such devices as electronic tape. As to the second sort of grammatical evidence, the grammar that is potential in speakers, it is much more difficult to identify, although it may not be the less revealing for that. It is to be sought in the ordered grammatical sense of those who know the language. No native speaker, however young, provided he can speak at all, needs to be told that words like *the* and *an* come before the noun, not after it. That is, grammar, the working of a language, exists in all users of the language, and if we wish, we should be able to derive it from them. As to the means of working, we can once more observe two, although they are not to be very sharply distinguished. Grammatical statements can be prepared more or less objectively, more or less subjectively, and if one endeavors to be objective, he can start with various sorts of criteria such as structure, sound, and meaning.

[As originally delivered, the lecture at this point included a survey of the growth of the conventional grammatical statement, perhaps sufficiently surveyed in the previous piece.]

That was the situation in English grammatical study, and in most Western study of language, until the current century, when, with Ferdinand de Saussure and others, something approaching a scientific means of measuring language was developed. It rests upon what we call the phoneme, which in turn rests upon the sense of sound and grammar in the users of the language. That is, a phoneme —by one definition, although there are others—is the smallest spread of sound that users of the language think of as a unit. It need not be one thing objectively; for example the sounds associated with the spelling *t*, that is, /t/, constitute a single phoneme in English because users of the language think of it as one thing. It is not, as anyone can prove who will say *time, bitter,* and *hut* before a mirror. He is likely to find, if he is an American speaker, that in *time* /t/, being initial, is made with the tip of the tongue nearly an inch back from the teeth, that the /t/ in *bitter,* being medial, is made with the tongue somewhat flattened and flipped against the ridge just back of the teeth, and that the terminal /t/ in *hut* is rather like the initial /t/ in *time,* but produced slightly more forward. All of these sounds could, of course, be described by their wave lengths, but doing so would be extremely complex. With the phoneme we have a relatively scientific unit of measurement, since it can be defined, but it is quite simple.

So now grammarians had the means of becoming relatively scientific. Instead of trying to determine the answers subjectively, they tried to work only from certainties and to go as far as they could with objectively measurable material. They had two certainties: the phoneme, which they could define, and structure, since phonemes always occur in some kind of order. By noticing the simplest combinations of phonemes they identified the morpheme, which is the smallest working unit of a language. For our purposes tonight we might equate a morpheme with a word, since what we call a word is usually a morpheme or a combination of relatively few morphemes.

Now the new grammarians—we may call them structural linguists and their study structural linguistics—had a method. They could start with phonemes, and by observing how phonemes combine, they could build these elements into sentences, or they could start with sentences and, by subjecting them to what are called *immediate constituent cuts,* break them up into a pattern of Chinese boxes and a string of phonemes. (To make an immediate constituent cut you take any piece of language and cut it into two where it would naturally break; that is, a clause becomes a subject and a predicate. Thereafter, each constituent is cut into its immediate constituents, and this process is continued until only phonemes remain.) This technique had its uses; it helped us record unwritten languages and it accelerated the learning of languages previously not well understood. How many GI's are now alive who would not have survived the last world war without structural linguistics will never be known, but the number is not small. It taught us things we had not suspected about parts of speech and about sentence patterns; it made us more aware of the permeating role of structure in language, but it never solved the basic problems of modern English grammar.

The structuralists had a good explanation for their limitations. They insisted they were scientists, working as scientists must work, going from the known to the unknown, following where their material leads. They had started at the surface of things with the only measurable, countable, and describal units of language they knew. Once they had worked through surface grammar they could approach deep grammar, and eventually they would be able, they hoped, to resolve all uncertainties in the whole language. Perhaps they will; as yet one can say only that they have not, that they have not done much to explore the more philosophic aspects of grammar, and that their system, however it may have helped in Borneo and Vietnam, has not done much to promote the teaching of the native language to the natives in the United States.

At this point we might pause a moment to note that the structuralists endeavored to use a scientific method as their approach. Like the chemist they studied elements and their structure. For materials they used a curious combination of both sorts of grammatical evidence that we have noticed. They worked on samples of preserved language, usually upon preserved oral language, since they studied stresses, pitches, and pauses, and the patterns of these, along with consonants and vowels. On the other hand, the phoneme with which they worked came out of the human mind, out of the grammatical awareness of the users of the language. It has no real, objective existence; it can be found only in the grammatical conviction of speakers and can be described by describing the language latent in them.

Structural study was only well embarked in this country, when it acquired a rival which I shall call generative grammar. Structural linguistics, we have observed, was curiously dual in its philosophy. The generative grammarians would have none of such compromises; they grounded their analysis frankly and wholly on the sense of grammaticality in the native speaker and endeavored to write out the rules by which a user of the language generates sentences. They used what are essentially the procedures of mathematics, trying to write out the most general rules that are true, and continuing this process until, hopefully, they will eventually make the most limited statements possible about the language. For example, they start with a formula like $S \rightarrow NP + VP$, which means that S (for sentence) can be written as NP (for noun phrase; that is, the subject and all that goes with it), plus VP (that is, the verb and all that goes with it). Next NP will be resolved into all its possible parts, step by step, and the same will be done for VP.

This procedure can readily become complicated, and it did, but the generative grammarians managed to simplify the whole procedure by becoming transformationalists. That is, they devised what they call transforms. They assumed that *I Love Lucy* can be transformed into *Lucy is loved by me*, which in one sense is probably unsound philosophy and in another is clumsy rhetoric, but it does help simplify the grammatical statement. Similarly, *The hat is stinking pink* can be transformed into *The stinking pink hat*. By such devices the transformationalists can start with five sorts of English sentences, which they call kernel sentences, and can presumably make all other possible structures into transforms of these. That is, they believe they can write out rules by which one can generate anything that anyone can write or speak in English.

That is the grammatical statement that is now attracting the most attention. Clearly, it has its uses; it produces a description consistent with itself. It has done much to simplify and dramatize the teaching of English at elementary levels, and more or less watered down, it is being written into many textbooks. In spite of the economy of transforms, however, at the more advanced levels, the transformational grammatical statement has become so complicated that nobody has been able to make much use of it, at least not yet. Furthermore, it suffers from at least one weakness; it rests upon the transform, but the transform has no existence, not even in the mind. Nobody who wants to exclaim, *The stupid moron!*, first constructs the kernel sentence *The moron is stupid* and then transforms this kernel sentence into what the transformationalists call a noun phrase. This is simply not the way minds work—at least not at any level we understand very well or comprehend consciously, although minds may work in some such way at unconscious levels, as some philosophical grammarians believe they do. Of course the grammatical statement need not follow the meanderings of the mind; materials are often best classified by characteristics other than the essential ones. We distinguish mollusks from men by the presence or absence of a spinal column, but surely the main difference between an Einstein and an oyster is not to be observed in a few vertebrae. If transforms simplify a grammatical statement we have every reason to use them, logical or illogical, but some of us who are impressed by the fact that grammar springs from minds have an enduring suspicion that in the end the most revealing grammatical statement will be one that reflects rather closely the working of minds through linguistic principles.

So, today, the transformational generative grammarians seem to be replacing the structural linguists, but the transformationalists too have acquired rivals. If Professor Noam Chomsky of Massachusetts Institute of Technology became the high priest of transformation, Professor Kenneth L. Pike of the University of Michigan is the Archbishop of Tagmemics. Now, you need not be abashed it you have never heard of a tagmeme or of tagmemics. *Tagmeme,* a coined word based upon Greek, might be defined as a hunk of something, and tagmemics might be called grammar by hunks, except that the tagmeme itself is rather less important than the approach, so that one might better call the method grammar by points of view. A tagmeme is defined as a basic unit of grammar, and in fact Pike first named his unit a *grameme,* on the analogy of *phoneme* and *morpheme,* terms which refer to basic units of sound and language. It is described as "a functional slot and the list of the mutually substitutable items that fill the slot."

That is, tagmemics is a string slot grammar, but it represents a considerable enlargement of the older slot theory. Any working portion of a sentence can be thought of as a slot. The formula we noted above, $S \rightarrow NP + VP$, is only a recognition of successive slots in a standard sort of sentence, subject plus verb, and usually plus complement. Transformational grammar, then, is a slot grammar plus transforms. Tagmemics is slot grammar enlarged to include all of language and broadened to include various ways of viewing language. A tagmeme includes everything that can go into a slot, including phonology and meaning, and on the analogy of allophones and allomorphs, tagmemes can be broken into *allotagmas*. On the sentence level tagmemics is conceived as including also the clause, phrase, word, and morpheme levels. But tagmemics is not limited to sentences; it includes also the larger and smaller units of language, everything up to the whole composition, and all of these are looked at in at least three ways, the terminology and the concepts borrowed from physics: particles, wave, and field. The first are what one would expect; particles are discrete units of language, morphemes for instance. Wave is harder to describe; Pike notices that waves have nuclei and margins, and they have been called "language units in their manifestation mode." The wave provides a dynamic view of language; in a very elementary way, wave appears when particles like segmental phonemes combine in speech; a pitch pattern is wave-like, although the concept of wave is larger than that of nonsegmental phonemes. Field provides a broad view of language. Thus tagmemics embodies an attempt to be at once inclusive and flexible. It is said to have been peculiarly useful in analyzing unwritten languages; as yet no detailed application to English has appeared in print, although Pike is known to be working on a manuscript.

At this writing, the most exciting new attempt to provide a grammatical statement goes under the name of stratificational grammar as expounded by Professor Sydney J. Lamb of Yale. Lamb's system has some of the advantages of several earlier attempts. Like structural linguistics, it gets down to specifics. It is generative in that it endeavors to describe how language comes to be through grammatical sense, but Lamb has little use for Chomsky or any of his works, including his transforms. It is like tagmemics in that it endeavors to analyze and describe language at all levels and in all manifestations. As Chomsky worked with mathematics and Pike with physics, Lamb has used computers; both the concepts and the terminology of electronics permeate his explanations. He reduces speech to impulses, and he makes use of relatively few concepts which he believes move through language—or at least through English and many other languages—at all levels, which he calls *and/or, upward/downward,* and *ordered/unordered.* With him, *upward* is toward meaning, that is, toward decoding linguistic signs, and *downward* is toward expression, toward encoding in linguistic signs. As for *and* and *or,* we all know that joining and choosing are linguistic operations; as for *ordered* and *unordered,* some linguistic phenomena fall into orderly patterns and others seem not to, at least from certain points of view. These six impulses can result in eight possible combinations, called *nodes,* as follows: unordered downward and, unordered downward or, unordered upward and, unordered upward or, ordered downward and, ordered downward or, ordered upward and, and ordered upward or. So viewed, language works on phonemic, morphemic, and lexemic levels, and can be graphed with what Lamb calls tactic, knot, and sign patterns. Inevitably, all this becomes complicated, and Lamb has been careful to insist that as yet his conclusions are "very tentative," but others have observed that stratification may prove to embody the breadth of tagmemics and the precision that has as yet been lacking in that discipline. In England something similar is being attempted by M. A. K. Halliday, called systemic grammar. Both Lamb and Halliday have relied on the Dane, Louis Hjelmslev, and his glossematics.

And now, something by way of summary and conclusion. First we might observe that there is no such thing as "the new grammar," if by that phrase you mean to imply that we formerly had a grammatical statement that was all wrong, and that we now have a new grammatical statement that is all right. But we do have new grammatical insight, new grammatical knowledge, and new grammatical promise. We have outgrown the old grammar; we have not yet grown into a new one. We have, I am sure for good and all, shaken ourselves loose from a grammatical stagnation, from a grammatical purblindness that kept us for decades from seeing anything much except what our ancestors had seen, at least some of which utilized little but linguistic myopia. If we do not yet have an entirely new grammatical statement, we do have great improvements in our grammatical approaches and we are developing an openness of mind that cannot but be good. Meanwhile, no one need fear what is called "the new grammar"; if it is not a new grammar, it does reflect a growing sense for language and a growing competence to deal with the basic tool of civilization. Neither need any teacher embrace the latest grammatical experiment desperately trusting that at long last the word has come down from Sinai. It has not, but American concepts of grammar and what to do about it are growing and broadening. And they will continue to grow.

━━◄{ 9. }►━━

Structural Linguistics:
Notes for a Devil's Advocate

The following piece was written for an institute at
Nebraska Wesleyan University about 1960 and published
as indicated below. It proved to be so prophetic that it
now has less interest than when it was written, and accordingly I have excised a survey of the state of structural
studies and a conclusion elaborating on the difficulties of
using structure as an approach in the classroom. What
remains may have some interest, however, all the more
because it can be applied with little adjustment to transformational grammar today and will probably apply to
tagmemics, stratification, and subsequent grammatical pro-
posals, if they ever become popular.

College English, XXIV (1962), 93–97.

For a decade or two everybody concerned with the application of linguistics to the teaching of English in this country has known where the angels stood. They stood on the side of the structuralists. Where else could they stand, poor things? They had their minds made up for them. After all, reforms were obviously needed in the English grammatical statement and the structuralists have been the most audible apostles, the St. Pauls who wasted not their talents crying in the wilderness. They had a new faith, and the faith obviously contained truth. But they have not always been received as apostles; their reception was not unlike that provided for Paul by "a certain orator named Tertullus," who called the apostle "a pestilent fellow and a mover of sedition." Perhaps few men entirely escape the pestilential, and there may have been structuralists among those who did not, but they did deserve to be heard, and not always did the Tertulluses of our profession grant them a ready hearing. Inevitably, the angels stood with them. But a time could come when the angels, discovering that the beleaguered apostles have become the aggressors, may feel that they must turn devil's advocate. I suspect that this time is upon us, and while I have no thought of attempting such advocacy, I would willingly supply a few notes for the advocate, against his arrival.

Meanwhile, bewildered traditionalists are turning to structure as the only remaining haven; this, I believe, we must regret. I see it in my students, in summer institutes, among teachers at NCTE conventions. They have discovered that the conventional grammatical statement is in part erroneous and at best inadequate, and they conclude, "So it's structural linguistics. There isn't anything else, is there?" I believe personally that there is a good bit else, although that is not the burden of this paper. I am suggesting that structural linguistics, in spite of its great and undeniable virtues as a linguistic tool, may not be as extensively useful in teaching English to the native speakers as many of its advocates either assume or assert. It warrants critical examination.

First let us consider the position of the pure structuralist, the scholar who studies structure in and for itself. I refer here to a linguist like Charles F. Hockett, who can and does say that he is seeking truth, and that the use of this truth, for teaching or anything else, is none of his business. He has only to assume that he has a valid method of working and significant material on which to work. Few competent students would question either of these assumptions, and the pure structuralist need make no others. He need not assume that the resulting grammatical statement will be the only valid grammar, or even that it will be the best grammatical statement, or that it has commercial, pedagogical, or any other practical use. Doubtless it has, but that is another question.

Thus the pure structuralist is logically unassailable. Not so his less fortunate colleague who endeavors to apply structural linguistics to the teaching of English to the native speakers of the language. He must assume various postulates, and I should estimate that devotees of teaching English by structural approaches, as they have developed during the last decade or so, make at least the following six assumptions:

1. *A scientific approach will be the best approach with which to understand and use language.* This is by no means a safe assumption. Science has not provided the best means to approach art, music, the dance, literature, theology, law, or in the past, philosophy, and it may not afford the best approach to language, particularly to the use of language, which is probably closer to art than it is to science.

2. *A study of structure based upon a study of sound will provide the most scientific description of language.* This, likewise, is dubious. No structural analysis of English yet reported is scientific in the sense that it is objective. Analysis rests upon such concepts as the phoneme, which has no real existence. It varies from language to language, from dialect to dialect, from time to time; it is a working concept, and apparently a very useful one, but let us not bemuse ourselves by trusting that it is scientific in any objective sense. Even in the hands of an expert it is not closely measurable; I recall having listened to a distinguished structuralist describing the phonemes

in English. The phonemes he was using as he spoke did not behave as he said in his speech they must behave. Of course description could be objective; if we had recorders enough, and tapes enough, and electric brains enough, and unemployed experts enough, we could analyze enough speech to say with some confidence what percentage of the population used a given unit of language in a given way, but the results would have changed by tomorrow, and would be too complex for most purposes.

3. *The best approach with which to understand language will be the best approach with which to teach it.* Again, the assumption is dangerous. Theoretical statements, useful though they are, should be applied only within the limits of their use. There may be no straight lines in the universe, but a bridge-builder who makes all lines deliberately crooked may find his bridge in the water. An oak door may be mostly air, but anyone who tries to walk through it may hurt his nose. Structural study is certainly important, but most truths have only limited uses, and structural study readily becomes so complicated that only specialists can deal with it; even they may require extensive time and cumbersome gadgets.

4. *We now have a sufficiently reliable understanding of linguistics in English so that we can formulate a practicable pedagogical statement.* Again, the assumption is unwarranted. It presumes that most competent authorities are in essential agreement, as they are about evolution or gravity, for example, however much they may differ as to details. We have no such agreement. At the moment we seem to have two emergent camps, those who believe in immediate constituents and those who rely upon transformations. Nor are these groups united; do you like Zellig Harris's transformations or Noam Chomsky's? Do you follow Bloch, or Trager, or Smith, or which combination of them when you cut for constituents? Since both of these approaches have appeared in recent years, a third and a fourth may bloom before this article can see print. Furthermore, most of the applications of structural approaches in English to date have relied heavily upon the work of Charles C. Fries, whom neither of the rising schools accepts. There is, of course, nothing wrong with this diversity; in the present state of our structural knowledge it is inevitable, or at least healthy, but it does not reassure one who is

faced with the problem of teaching one truth, with one philosophy, and one set of terms and procedures to bewildered youth.

5. *The study of the grammar of the native language provides an essential, and probably the best means of improving the use of the native tongue.* Once more, the assumption is not obviously valid; many good writers know little formal grammar. Many of us believe that any study of language indirectly promotes the use of language, whatever the method of study, whether by comparative grammar or Scrabble. Studying a foreign language inevitably involves some study of the grammar of that language, but most school systems do not much utilize the study of the native grammar. The American system apparently makes a fetish of this. Numerous tests have not demonstrated that teaching the conventional grammatical statement has much impact upon writing; of course the fault here may be that the conventional statement is inadequate, and again it may not. Besides, structural linguistics, by the admission of the best structuralists, as yet provides no more than what is sometimes called surface grammar. Deep grammar by structural approaches is for the future, if ever.

6. *One method of teaching the use of the native language will be best for all ages.* Again, the assumption is dubious; it is spectacularly not true for almost any other subject one can think of, and why should it be for the native language? Who would try to teach quantum theory as he teaches a fourth grader to multiply? Nor need uncertainty rest solely upon analogy. The study of grammar obviously has more to do with the study of usage than with the study of prosody, and if structural study is important for prosody, it is important in a different way.

Now we might remind ourselves that any belief which rests upon a dubious assumption is suspect, and that any belief which relies upon two interreliant dubious assumptions is more than twice as suspect. Here we have six dubious assumptions, all more or less interreliant.

--◄ 10. ►--

A Simpleminded Look
at Grammar and Language

Written at the invitation of the Conference on College Composition and Communication, this paper was read at the meeting of the organization in Miami Beach in 1969 and printed in the organization's official journal.

College Composition and Communication, XX (1969), 181–86.

--ᵃ{ Everybody knows what language is, but in anything like a final analysis, nobody knows what grammar is. We may not be able to define language, but we all use it, we know when we are using it, and we recognize it when we encounter it. Not so, grammar. It has long been the bane of the young, partly because they cannot find out what it is, and the doctors have fared little better. They cannot agree how it works, how it is related to men and mental processes, or even how one should go about studying it, once it can be identified and defined, defined in the sense that limits can be set to it.

The word *grammar*, after the waywardness of vocabulary, has meant many things at various times and places. Apparently it comes from a Greek root associated with art, including literary art, and the word could mean anything written. Whoever penned *Piers Plowman* wrote that grammar "grounde is of alle," but Robert Burns, irked with an adverse critic supposedly guilty of grammatical leanings, addressed him as follows:

> thou squeaking dissonance of cadence; thou pimp of gender; thou scape-gallows from the land of syntax; thou scavenger of mood and tense; thou murderous accoucheur of infant learning; thou *ignis fatuus,* misleading the steps of benighted ignorance; thou pickle-herring in the puppet-show of nonsense.

Burns seems to be implying that grammar, whatever else it may be, is infantile. Presumably this is a transferred use from the concept of the grammar school, but whatever the source, the word *grammar* came to refer to elements and to matters elementary, as it does in Thomas Fuller's observation that "Manly sports are the Grammar of Military performance."

Of late, this last has not represented the trend in either grammatical teaching or grammatical thinking. Nelson Antrim Crawford

75

quoted a Kansas farmer as saying, "That sure is a great school. It's practical. They don't teach no goddam grammar there." Whatever the relationship of grammar to perdition, many a teacher of composition, while abjuring the farmer's terminology, might have seconded his intent. They would say that instruction should be practical, at least to the extent that it teaches something that is of some use, and that grammar as it has usually been taught has not been very useful for composition.

Furthermore, the grammatical statements supplied by scholars have not been simple or elementary, particularly not of late. Even the traditional description was so complex that it became intelligible in any real sense only in monumental tomes like those by Poutsma and Kruisinga, and these differed from one another. Structural linguistics rests upon simple principles, but it rapidly becomes so complex that only experts can decide where allophones are to be assorted among phonemes. These allophonic relationships are constantly shifting in any language, and fine distinction must always be arbitrary. Transformational grammar, although it has among its purposes discovering unity in apparent diversity and although its broader principles reveal a simplicity at once practical and beautiful, is becoming so complex that we do not as yet have a transformational description of English, and when we get one, it is likely to be so involved that instructors in Freshman English—not to mention their compatriots in elementary and secondary schools—may find little use for it. More recent approaches like tagmemics and stratification offer intriguing vistas, partly because they promise to merge grammar into a comprehensive statement about language, but they cannot at this time be charged with anything approaching simplicity, except in their broader statements, where they rely on generalizations which most of us find nearly meaningless except as they are refined through detail. That a working unit of language may be describable as *upward ordered and* or as *downward unordered or* may be linguistically exciting, and may even become pedagogically useful, once these generalizations can be reified through language in use, but such detail is as yet only sketchily available, and one fears that when we do have practical application it will not be pie in the sky for the beginner.

Thus, perhaps especially for the teacher of composition, there may be virtue in asking the simplest questions we can devise about language, including grammar, and in endeavoring to content ourselves with relatively simple answers. At the outset we might ask of what language is composed. We could supply many answers, depending upon the basis we select for analysis, but one of the simplest would be this: all languages we have discovered or have heard about seem to comprise two sorts of things, linguistic units and a means of handling these units so that they have enlarged use. The first are what we call vocabulary, whether we conceive that the vocabulary is made up of words, of syllables, or morphemes and phrases, or what not; the second includes understandings, practices, and devices for handling these units, what we call grammar.

These two, whether we call them parts of language, aspects of language, or whatever, do not occur in pure state—in fact, very little, if anything in language occurs in pure state. Consider the linguistic units. Clearly they are involved in meaning, particularly if we define meaning very broadly to include semantic impact upon the hearer or reader, an aid to thought or expression on the part of the user, a need like making an impression on others, satisfying an emotional lack, performing a ritual, and the like. But these linguistic units inevitably become involved in grammar, even though they may undergo no change in form or participate in any structure. Locutions like *No, Help! Okay,* and *Really?* involve grammar, a minimal sort of grammar perhaps, and one revealed in part by phonological patterns in speech and by isolation in writing, but still grammar. A word like *help* normally occurs in some associative pattern, as in *Help was a long way off,* or *He will help if he can,* and we know that it will participate in the grammar of such sequences. When it occurs in no sequence it must inevitably involve within itself the sorts of grammar that become possible by isolation, the grammar of only very few uses, that of an entry in a dictionary, or an imperative, or interrogative, and the like, but still grammar, since through isolation we know something other than what we would know if the linguistic unit was used in context.

Similarly, grammar can have only a limited existence except in conjunction with linguistic units. We all know that sentence patterns can be filled with nonsense syllables, and theoretically one should be able to hum sentence patterns, although doing so with any accuracy is not easy. Some grammar can appear within linguistic units themselves. Inflections may provide almost nothing we could call meaning, being mainly concerned with revealing grammar, and a linguistic unit like *of* may serve as a synthetic device, being almost exclusively grammatical. Other units like *in, by, and,* and *not* may be extensively involved in analytic grammar, while retaining more or less meaning. Most of the grammar of a sentence, however, will result from the interaction of the parts of the sentence, whether these are bound or free morphemes, words, or linguistic units less than words. That is, grammar seems to be a set of devices and understandings to enhance meaning beyond whatever is possible within the linguistic units themselves—to make such a statement we shall of course have to recognize isolation as embodying a sort of zero interaction. A matron may shout *Girls!* and to a person in danger one might shout *Run,* and we have seen that these locutions possess grammar, but immediately if they are juxtaposed the grammar changes. We observe quite different grammar in *Girls run,* with an enlarged or at least a refined meaning, and if we add more linguistic units to interact with these, we get still more refined meanings, as in *Some girls run up big bills getting themselves prettified at the hairdresser's,* and *Delinquent girls may readily run out of plausible excuses for leaving home.*

We might notice somewhat more particularly the role of interaction in such sentences. Consider the witticism, "Life is one silly thing after another; love is two silly things after one another." Formally and structurally the two halves of this sentence are similar. The patterns of immediate-constituent cuts in the two would be nearly identical, and the differences would not be very revealing of the actual differences between the two sentences. Likewise, if one were to use the generative rules of phrase structure he would derive a description both uncertain and inadequate. The second clause uses a plural, *things,* and the determiner *two* as against the determiner *one,* but these slight differences give little indication of the total difference, in this sentence, between *one silly thing,* apparently a trivial event, and *two silly things,* apparently enamored human beings. The second clause also contains the linguistic unit *one* between the units *after* and *another,* and this intrusion of the word *one* would somewhat alter the generative trees for the two clauses, but scarcely enough to reflect what happens. In the first sentence *after another* is spatial, whether we call it adjectival or adverbial; in the second clause *after* becomes rather more verbal, a shift which becomes more apparent if we redraft the clause to read *Love is two silly things going for one another,* although *after one another* could also be considered adjectival. That is, the interaction of the linguistic units in the sentence not only determines the impact, the meaning, of the sentence, but it determines the use and hence the meaning of the units themselves.

Or consider another sentence made up of two clauses, a current advertising slogan, "You can take Smokies out of the country, but you can't take the country out of Smokies." Here, except for the inclusion of a negative in the second clause, there is no formal difference at all in the units of the two sequences, but most of the words mean differently and relate differently with the differences in word order. Presumably *you* and *Smokies* are essentially the same in both clauses, but all the other linguistic units, even to the article *the,* have different grammar and mean differently in the two sequences. *The country* of the first clause is not at all *the country* of the second, and whether you treat *take out of* as a verb or whether you treat it as a verb plus part of a modifier, none of the units *take, out,* and *of* either means or functions in the same way in the two clauses. That is, if we wish, we could construct a grammar of modern English which would recognize meaning as an important end of grammatical practices, and interaction among linguistic units as an important means.

We must, of course, recognize that no known grammar works with only one grammatical device, that we can devise various grammatical statements depending upon the assumptions with which we start, and that hence grammarians, in preparing a description of a language, must always prefer some assumptions to others. The older grammarians assumed the primacy of the parts of speech; the structural linguists preferred to rely upon structure and to avoid meaning; the transformationalists have relied upon generative rules on the analogy with mathematics, as these rules could be supplemented with transformations. We are now being introduced to the possibilities of stratification in language, and the concepts of particle, wave, and field. These approaches have provided adequate pure grammatical statements or they give promise of doing so, but as yet none has provided an entirely satisfactory applied grammar of the sort likely to be useful in the teaching of composition.

I am suggesting, then, that a grammatical statement could be developed by recognizing the importance of meaning in language; such a grammatical description would rely so heavily upon the role of interaction among linguistic units that we might well call it an interactive grammar. I am further suggesting that since meaning and interaction seem to describe pretty readily the working of the human mind when the mind works by means of American English —more conveniently for example than do structure or transformations, whether or not more precisely—such a grammatical statement might prove the most useful in teaching composition, or at the least, more useful than most of the grammatical statements we have as yet been offered. Such a statement would resemble in its outlines at least some of what we already recognize as the working of function, but I surmise that an approach through interaction may provide us with a more revealing description than has yet appeared through the rather patchy attention thus far accorded to concepts of function.

At this point we might pause to ask ourselves what pertinence, if any, these deliberations have for our present concerns. Personally, I am not sure they are of primary significance. I have become convinced that as teachers of composition we should be much more occupied with long-range objectives than with short-range goals. I have become convinced, also, that a broad knowledge of the nature and working of language helps students learn to profit from the use of language, and the great growth of linguistic readers in composition courses seems to attest that the belief is not unique with me. I have become convinced, also, that as teachers of composition we have trusted grammar too much and rhetoric too little, that we need a new rhetoric more than we need a new grammar, and that when we get a modern rhetorical statement the teaching of composition will improve. I have been impressed, also, by the overwhelming evidence that the grammar of the native language is mainly learned unconsciously, that natives can learn to use the native speech with competence and even with artistry although blessed with little or no formal instruction in the native grammar, that as a people we have been much misled by confusing the needs of learning a foreign tongue with the needs of learning native speech. I have been impressed, further, with our tardiness in developing what is now called psycholinguistics, and our still greater tardiness in applying what little we have discovered about language learning, and I question whether organizations like the NCTE and the CCCC should have spent so much time talking about grammar and structure and so little talking about vocabulary and meaning.

The fact remains, however, that if the importance of teaching grammar as a part of teaching writing has been grossly and persistently exaggerated, presumably it has use. Even Robert Burns, part of whose anathema I quoted earlier, included as one of his epithets, "thou carpenter, mortising the awkward joints of jarring sentences," and if this joiner's work is not the most laudable of all auctorial activities, I surmise that most of us would agree that it represents a worthy concern, practical even in the sense in which the Kansas farmer was using the word *grammar*. And something more can be said. I suspect that the principal use of grammar in composition courses is this, that an understanding of the grammatical working of the language helps the writer to develop a surer grasp of the essentials of strong and precise sentence structure. Even in writing sentences, as I have implied earlier, rhetorical questions tend to take precedence over grammatical questions, both in choosing and in handling structures at any but the most elementary levels, but writing has so much to do with wholes and with the interreliance of parts that grammar, also, has its use.

For example, grammar emphasizes the working of the subject and verb in predication, and sound predication is the heart of English prose structure. Just here, I should say, transformational grammar exposes one of its signal weaknesses as a teaching device; no doubt, grammatically, the passive is a transform of the active, but rhetorically the passive and the expletive constructions are anything but equivalents of the active. This is not to say, of course, as some texts do, that the active voice provides the strong way of writing and the passive and expletive the weak ways of writing, but it is to say that these three basic sentence sorts in English have very different rhetorical uses, differences that are obscured rather than revealed by the concept of the transform. The semantic and interactive approaches, on the other hand, illuminate the working of predication, especially the working of complex predicates involving verb sets, adverbial structures that blend imperceptibly into complements, and the like.

Similarly, one of the glories of the English sentence is to be observed in the variety and subtlety of subordination in modern structures. Students of composition can profit from much more study of subordination than they are usually offered, and from study that reveals rather than obscures what happens when lesser structures relate to the kernel of the sentence and to one another. The conventional statement that an adverb modifies a verb, an adjective, or another adverb is essentially confusing as well as factually inaccurate, but chopping the parts of a predicate into the leavings of immediate-constituent cuts does not help much more, nor does the hanging of modifiers on generative trees. The new generative diagrams are almost as rigid as the old parsing diagrams, whereas a grammar that is of much use in the teaching of composition would reveal the fluidity, not the rigidity of modern American English.

Naturally, I cannot expound a detailed interactive grammar in brief compass, but I shall suggest lines along which I seem to see such a grammar moving, and to this end I shall try to formulate fundamental principles:

1. Complex structures may, but need not, be derivable from simple structures having some of the same linguistic elements. As we have seen above, structures like *Girls run up bills* and *Girls run out of excuses* are not the same structures as *Girls run.*

2. Linguistic units interact, and it will be useful to recognize various sorts of interaction as functions that may be served within the sentence. Perhaps the most readily recognized functions are three: nexus, which includes the working together of being subject, being verb, and being complement; modification; and showing relationships not involved in nexus and not well described as modification.

3. Any of these functions may be subsumed under one linguistic unit, for example by one word, but all of a function need not be included within one linguistic unit, and any linguistic unit need not be involved in only one function.

In fact, in complex prose, one should not expect that most

functions will be confined to only one linguistic unit, nor that most linguistic units will be involved in only one function. In *Girls run,* "girls" is involved in being subject, and there is not much else it can be involved in, and "run," although it may be involved in more than one function, subsumes these within itself, but most communication does not take place on the childish level of *Girls run.* Even in a relatively simple sentence like *Gaggles of geese floated on the pond* most of the words are involved in more than one function, participate in more than one grammatical action or interaction. Both "gaggles" and "geese" are involved in being subject within nexus, but they are also involved in interactive relationships that we might roughly call modification. "Floated" is involved in being verb, but it also participates in our conception of the geese at the moment, so that we must recognize that it, like most of the words conventionally called verbs, is involved also in modification. Similarly, "on the pond" would conventionally be recognized as being involved in modifying "floated," but it also affects our concept of the "gaggles of geese," and it is at the same time concerned with the predication that was started with these words, as can be seen if we make substitutions in the sentence so that it reads, *Officers of the company floated a loan.* Without words like "gaggles of geese" and "on the pond" we do not know how "floated" is functioning, or even what it means in the limited dictionary sense.

In short, as a devotee of language, I am delighted with the fresh concepts and the intriguing new approaches with which grammarians are providing us these days, but I surmise that we could develop a grammatical statement that would be more useful in the teaching of composition than are any now being offered us.

—⊰ 11. ⊱—

Language History,
and What, If Anything,
to Do about It

This paper was written at the request of the Idaho Conference of Teachers of English, and read at one of their conventions, probably in 1966. Most of what is said here has been surveyed more elaborately in lectures printed above, but perhaps not applied so directly to the needs of teachers, particularly the needs of those with somewhat limited backgrounds in language. So far as I recall, nobody ever suggested that he wanted to publish the piece nor did I suggest that anybody should.

Ladies and Gentlemen: You must all have had this experience, that having been asked to speak to somebody about something, you have wondered why you should speak to anybody about anything. Are you not, you ask yourself, conniving in a sort of imposture, like being fed questions on a quiz program or pretending you believe that strontium ninety may provide a vitamin-rich diet for growing boys and girls. You know quite well that machinery will be put in gear to discomode a hotel, to agitate the public prints at least mildly, to assemble people, under what pretenses and under what hopes you can only surmise. I may confess that I raised such questions when I was asked to tell my fellow English teachers in fifteen minutes what they should teach of the history of language. And having raised such questions I did not do very well for answers. I tried for a handsome trinity, but apparently there are few good answers why anybody should ever do what I am attempting now. For what the answers may be worth, here they are.

Billions of men and women, living and dead, have been speaking thousands of languages, living and dead, for tens of thousands, perhaps hundreds of thousands of years. At any one moment the linguistic phenomena produced by these millions of speakers have been for all practical purposes infinite; as the old song has it the speech contained more lies—as well as more linguistic phenomena —than "the cross-ties on the railroad, or the stars in the skies." I am asked to tell you what should be taught the unsuspecting young out of this vast agglomeration, the history of language. Mercifully, most of it is dead and gone, but as you well know, the shelves of our libraries bulge, and they continue to burgeon, with the linguistic phenomena which have not as yet escaped the ravages of fire, indolence, and hazy memory. If I manage to say but little this morning the fault will surely not rise from paucity of material.

Now for my second defense, and regretfully I confess that it is negative—though I have been told that a speaker should never be negative—I shall not tell you that mine is the most important subject. Frankly, I feel that telling young people what language seems to be is more important than telling them what it has been. Most young people do not know what language is—as a matter of fact, I don't either, but let us pass that point—and I know of nothing better for them to do than to try to find out. Thus if I must defend my speech I can say only this, that sometimes one understands the present by studying the past. One might notice in passing that some subjects are essentially worth studying and some more worth teaching. I take it that brushing one's teeth and driver education are subjects which, within limits, are worth teaching, but they are certainly poor subjects for research. Conversely, the history of language is a fasinating subject for research, but it does not follow that teaching the stuff has an equally laudable purpose. Personally, I rather think it has; deep down where I feel most human I have a persistent gnawing notion that teachers ought frankly say to the world, "Our business is to show people how to have fun, enduring fun with the great ideas of all time," but I fear this notion would be unwelcome to school boards and boards of regents, and I suggest it now only because I am confident I am among friends who will not betray me.

Let us assume, then, that this is true, that we can promote our understanding of the way language works now by studying the manner in which it has worked in previous centuries. Here, perhaps, we need one reservation, that if we are to teach the history of language at all, we should teach the most important facts about the history of language, not the errors and the trivia. This has not always been the approach. Noah Webster, who supposed that language had first appeared on the plains of Chaldee, believed that the first words were verbs and that all other parts of speech had sprung from them. This belief of his rested in part upon his supposed observation that the word *if* came from an early form of the word *give*. Of course it did not, but he presumably lived and died without discovering his error; he was not, as a matter of fact, notably alert at discovering his errors. Similarly, many apologists for language have postulated that the original tongue was Hebrew, and that any small child abandoned among a few gently-disposed and nursing female sabretooth tigers would grow up babbling Hebrew. I need not remind you that no known child has done so. Some devotees of the classical tongues have declared that Latin and Greek are better languages than English and French because they are more exact, or that Italian is a better language than Spanish because it is more melifluous. If such statements have any foundation in fact, the foundation is highly impressionistic not to say dubious, and I, at least, have little concern with teaching it. If we are to teach anything from the history of language to secondary-school and lower-division college students, we should be teaching facts which can be determined and inferences which reach right down to the soul of mankind, where language and society work together in making man what he seems to be.

Perhaps we can agree, then, that if we teach the history of language or the history of the English language to younger students, we must describe major tendencies, we must restrict ourselves to clearly demonstrable fact, and we should select fact not for itself alone, but because it provides a test-tube case, because it suggests what language seems to be and how it works. Obviously, the linguistic phenomena that best satisfy this trinity of requirements may not be certain and obvious; not all students would agree upon them. I assume, therefore, that here *I* come in, that our chairman has asked me to give at least one man's guess as to what out of all the welter of language phenomena is most worth teaching the young.

My choice, then, and I concede it is a personal one, embraces the following: 1) language has grown and branched in such a way that it appears in families; 2) vocabulary as we know it has come from the users of a language; 3) language is always changing and our own grammar has undergone a revolution in historic times; and, 4) borrowing is a fundamental fact in language as in life, and our own language is distinguished by the richness of the Greek-Latin-French cultural stream. I can do little more this morning than identify these four.

Take the first, that languages appear in families. Without this, the concept of cognates and of etymology in the sense in which we now conceive it are impossible. Fortunately, for us as pedagogues, this is an exciting idea. Youngsters are entranced by the notion that the languages of the world fit into great families, with brothers and sisters and ancestors; that their own language can be traced back time out of mind through various reconstructed tongues to Indo-European; that English has a common ancestor with other languages that now seem as different as Greek, French, and Russian; that words like *father* and *paternal* are reunited in English again, after thousands of years of wandering through various branches of the Indo-European language family; that *to win* and the name for the godess of love can be traced to a long dead word for striving, discernible vaguely through the mists of the millennia. I suggest that children should be taught something about the concept of families and descent in language, and particularly something of the relationship of English within the family of Indo-European languages. As a matter of fact, it does no harm if they learn a few Indo-European bases, and some of the words that have descended from these bases. Youngsters find this exciting, although the subject is apparently not much taught. I find that any colleague who can name ten Indo-European bases is a rare *pou-, *pou- being the Indo-European base from which a number of our words for *birds* have developed, *fowl* and *pullet,* for example.

Now for the second fundamental fact, that much of any language as it is in use is made by the users of the language. This is not, of course, exclusively a matter of history; it is going on all the time, but it can be well observed in the history of words. Notice *square,* for instance; it is related to the Latin *quattuor* through French, and presumably responded to our need for a name for four-sided, four-cornered objects, which have been becoming more common since Roman times. Many American towns were laid out with the central block empty for a park, which became the Square. But as you know, Times Square is anything but square, and a recent description of an Italian town written by an American refers to its "triangular square." We have needed a name for an open space in a town and city, and we have made over the use of the word *square* to fill our need, whether or not the space is square. That is, we were making language here, as we always are. By what processes do we make it? By a good many, obviously, including particularization and generalization. Students may appropriately study these social and psychological processes by which we make language, and the manner in which we have made new words out of old ones and have adapted old words to new uses should provide as graphic evidence as anything.

Third, I feel we should teach that language is always changing, and again, to observe the change we usually have to look back a way, either to notice the change as in variant spellings, or to account for the change, as in dialects. Personally, I commend noticing what has happened to the grammar of English. As most of you will know, the English language has changed since early Anglo-Saxon times from a highly inflected language to a highly analytic language. This study has the great advantage that it gives students some glimpse of what grammar is, of how broad, subtle, and pervasive it is; many students are prone to assume that grammar is concerned mainly with such trivialities as whether one may or must not end a sentence with a preposition. A glimpse at the changes in pronunciation from Anglo-Saxon to modern English times would of course serve as well as grammar to suggest the extent and quality of change in language, but such study requires more by way of preparation and apparatus, both for the teacher and the student. At least some changes in grammar are obvious; Anglo-Saxon words are thick with inflectional endings, in some instances with rather long ones. Anyone can see them, and anyone can see also that modern English does very well without them, and that when he compares an ending-language with a no- or few-ending language he has grammar visible, right there before his eyes.

Lastly, I suggest that we teach the great fact of borrowing, of which the borowing of language is a salient result and in which the borrowing of language is a key requisite. Apparently, wherever peoples are in association, they borrow, and the essential foundation of western civilization is this, that Mediterranean culture flowed north and west. As it flowed, it carried language with it, and thus the swelling Greek-Latin-French stream of borrowing into English provides at once a basic statement for the understanding of much of our language and one of the splendid examples for all time of the nature and significance of borrowing in life and language.

And now, if I have timed myself accurately, I have run over by about half a minute. But after all, time is of the essence in language as in law, and this paper is concerned with time and language. Anyhow, who would be so miserly as to begrudge half a minute to the great English language?

⟶⊰ 12. ⊱⟵

Seen but not Heard;
Language Learning
and Language Teaching

During 1968, at the invitation of the National Council of Teachers of English and of the respective host institutions, the following lecture was read at the University of Alaska, Fairbanks; Alaska Methodist University, Anchorage; Merry Mount College, Yankton, S.D.; Gadsden Junior College, Gadsden, Ala., the Red Bluff and Mendocino County School systems in California, and to some other groups. It stemmed from my observation that, although the assumption had long been that children learn grammar only after they have started to learn words and have linguistic units to put together, they in fact learn grammatical patterns much earlier, notably in the first year of their lives. At about the time I was making my observations, several other scholars had been attracted to the possibility that grammatical learning might come earlier than had been assumed. When I wrote my lecture I was unaware of this new research, and indeed, even at this writing, very little has been published along such lines.

The Range of English: NCTE Distinguished Lectures, 1968 (Champaign, Ill., 1968), pp. 75–103. This version contained bibliographical footnotes.

—⚬❦ [For brevity I have excised an introduction in which I reminded my auditors of a hoary but relatively unconfirmed adage that children should be seen but not heard.]

The last century has witnessed a revolution in our attitudes toward children and in our estimation of their importance. We now study children with care and sympathy, partly for the sake of the children, partly because we have become aware that children can help us understand both human nature and human society, and since my subject this evening is language, I should add that this fascination with the young has extended to their language, and especially to language learning. This is now a lively subject for research, and as results we have excellent books and monographs treating the acquisition of both vocabulary and grammar from about the third year of a child's life, but I have lately become convinced that most studies I have seen are somewhat damaged because they dealt with children already too mature, or because they have been made by people who, however much they knew about children, did not know much about language. But before I detail my conclusions let me present some of my evidence.

First, I wish to abjure any pretensions to having been scientific. I respect science and I would willingly study language scientifically, insofar as I am able, but I blundered into the evidence I expect to present to you, and once I had started collecting material I could not go back and assemble data in any controlled way. Children stubbornly refuse to live their lives over again, even in the interests of science. Nor do I expect to embark upon a scientific study; at my age I can scarcely devote a lifetime to the linguistic concerns of infants, and my interests being what they are, I am not likely to make even a good start. Nor shall I cast the aura of science over my observations; since my collecting resulted from a highly personal relationship, and since the results may have been colored by that relationship, I shall deal frankly with human beings in a human situation.

The subject of my observations is one of my granddaughters, Hanna Jo Hunt. Circumstances dictated that I was to see but little of her during the first six months of her life, but thereafter for a time I saw her every week or two in either her home or ours, although nothing she did attracted my curiosity as a student of language until she was about a year old. She is a good-natured, outgoing, chattery child, and by that time she would babble extensively at anyone to whom she had become accustomed. In line with my belief that children should be treated like human beings, I talked with her, using words and constructing sentences, since I did not trust myself to speak naturally otherwise. Sometime during this process I noticed that we were carrying on conversations. Hanna would ask a question, in her babble sounds, which I would answer in English. Of course I did not know what the question concerned, because Hanna had used nothing in these discourses that could be recognized as English words, but I postulated a subject for her question and answered accordingly. I would then ask her a question, a real question, to which she would reply, sometimes promptly, sometimes with a show of deliberation, using the sentence patterns of what were obviously various sorts of answers in modern English.

This intrigued me, and I started listening to Hanna's speech as phonemic patterns. By this time she had acquired many of the segmented sounds of modern English, both vowels and consonants, although by no means all of them. I observed nothing that could be called a morpheme or a word used with any consistency for an apparent purpose, although I should add that my observations were sketchy enough so that I could have missed such signals. Her grammatical patterns, on the other hand, were unmistakable, and she commanded all of the more common ones without hesitation and with no evidence of difficulty. Obviously she was having fun; in fact, she used her language only when she was happy. Any kind of distress led only to silence or wails, but when she was enjoying herself she could command all the sentence patterns adequate to her life. She could greet you saying the equivalent of "Hi, Bud," or a somewhat more restrained, "Hello, nice you came." She could attract attention ("Hey, see what I'm doing,") and make expository observations, some of them rather lengthy and accompanied with pauses as though she were thinking. She could distinguish, using pitch, stress, and juncture patterns, the differences between various sorts of imperatives. What I took to be the equivalent of "Give me a bottle," shared something with an imperative like, "Notice that my sister is really very funny," but was also distinguished from it. She could even "read" a book; that is, she could chatter while turning the pages of a book, but so far as I could observe she was much less sure of herself when "reading," probably because she heard less reading than speaking and because the various members of the family who read to her did so in quite different pitches and patterns.

This "language" of Hanna's gave evidence of being a self-contained system, although it must have grown from the sentence patterns she had heard in her home, which would have been mainly adult patterns. Her sisters are respectively some ten and twelve years older than she, of much more than average literacy and at that time she was not regularly seeing children of her own age. So far as I could observe, her use of her language patterns was impeccable. She was never at a loss for grammatical sequences, and she seemed to use them with a high degree of consistency— granted, of course, that one did not always know what she meant to say. Obviously, her imitative powers were very great, especially, it would seem, in her ability to reproduce pitch, stress, and juncture unconsciously. All the sounds she used in her language were involved within these patterns. Meanwhile, she was beginning to use a few words. I heard *Mommy* and *bobbu* (for bottle), but these she never used in her babble language. They were isolated cries, not much more than signs, occasioned by immediate need.

In general the situation seems clear enough. In the first year of her life Hanna had learned a number of what probably amounted to segmental phonemes—at least she had learned sounds, and she seemed to use them phonemically. She was still having difficulty with many sounds she had heard, and her ability to imitate isolated sounds was limited, partly no doubt because of short verbal memory, and partly because she as yet had too little control of her tongue to make possible the sounds requiring agile and precise tongue movement. She could combine sound, but it is doubtful that any sounds, whether individual or combined, represented much more than material she could put into patterns. Meanwhile she had learned pitch, stress, and juncture with remarkable accuracy and some variety, and I assume that these suprasegmental sequences included all the patterns she heard regularly in her home.

During the next few months, I observed some increase in the complexity of Hanna's sentence patterns. She had learned simple coordination and would join what appeared to be nouns, modifiers, and clauses, the latter often with pauses between them, and I suspect that she was here imitating, even to the apparently thoughtful breaks, her eldest sister, a speculative youngster who would sometimes offer quite mature observations. She had learned subordination before the noun; she could say the equivalent of *an old man,* but I did not isolate patterns like *a very decrepit, pitiful old man,* presumably because the conversation in the household did not much run to extensive subordination patterns. Naturally, with only one adult in the home—Hanna's mother was at that time divorced— and the remaining members relatively young, Hanna heard only simple structures with any consistency, but her facility in acquisition was such that one must assume she would have learned any pattern, however complex, if she had heard it enough.

Meanwhile Hanna's mother and her sisters were deliberately teaching her words. A sister would say, "See the kitty, Hanna. Say *kitty.*" "Kitty." "What is that, Hanna?" No answer. "It's a kitty. Say *kitty,* Hanna." "Kitty." That is, by now Hanna could say most brief words in immediate, direct imitation, but she could say these words only by repeating them immediately after someone. They did not enter into her language, and they were never said with the sentence patterns of conversation. She would say *"Kitty"* with the imperative pattern that her sister had used in "Say *kitty,* Hanna," never with the pattern, "The kitty wants some milk."

During the next few months, say until Hanna was nearly a year and a half old, she was simultaneously developing four aural systems that I could distinguish. One answered to immediate need; limited in vocabulary and almost innocent of grammar, it consisted of cries, more or less urgent. The original *Mommy* and *bobbu* had been joined by a few others—her sisters' names, along with *read* and *dinner*—but this system grew very slowly both in extent and complexity. The others Hanna had made into games, which I shall call for convenience the Whazzat Game, the Ritual Game, and the Playing Grown-up Game. The first of these games probably grew out of the "Say kitty" pattern. Hanna had now learned the names of various objects around the home, particularly those that could be observed in children's books or in mail order catalogues, and during this period any adult that appeared would be set upon by Hanna, dragging a picture book or a catalogue.

To play the Whazzat Game, Hanna sat on the adult's lap—or stood nearby if she was not certain of the adult—and both looked at the book. If Hanna said "Whazzat?" the adult was supposed to name the object. If the adult pointed to a familiar object and said, "What's that?" Hanna would answer, "Daddy," or "fishie," or "clock," or whatever might be appropriate. She would reply promptly if she had a word for the object and part of the game seemed to be to answer as quickly as possible. She used the pattern of her sister in "Say *kitty*," and she would do this interminably with great delight. In fact, she seemed to prefer the mail order catalogues because they permitted the interlocutor to point to twenty clocks in succession, and she could say "Clock," almost instantaneously. Never, however, did she use the pattern that she would have used had she been saying, "The clock has stopped." This was a game with its own rules, and it had nothing to do with either her cries in need or her language used for conversation, that is, with the quite separate game of playing Grown-up. She used the pattern of "Say kitty," which was the pattern associated with this game, whoever was doing the pointing. During this game she was not averse to learning to respond to previously unknown objects, to a shotgun or a swimming suit, but clearly she preferred the same object, available in many variations, so that she could respond with zealous rapidity to a series of clocks or to a sequence of clocks and daddies pointed at alternately.

In view of the paucity of her general understanding, her grasp of what she conceived to be the central idea behind a group of related and namable objects was amazing. She could recognize a photograph of a fish, a painting of a fish, a caricature of a fish, a fish design on an ashtray, and jewelry in a form suggestive of a fish. Presented with a fishlike form in a medium strange to her she might hesitate a bit, but she seldom missed, and she was apparently pleased with herself when she recognized a fish under a strange guise, as though this was part of the game and she was winning.

That is, this was a game using answers; it had nothing to do with communication. It did, however, if I am right, have much to do with a developing sense of language. Hanna seemed here to be going from observed details to a formalization behind these details. She was developing, one assumes unconsciously, a sense for symbol. In no other way can I explain the fact that a blob on a ceramic ashtray was "Fishie!"—and Hanna was in no doubt about this—whereas to an untutored, literal eye it would have looked more like a hump of melting ice cream than anything dragged from the sea. Since I was not watching for the growth of a symbol sense in Hanna I cannot say how early she developed it, but I did note her awareness of the fish as a symbol by the time she was fifteen months old.

A somewhat similar set of responses I have included in what I call the Ritual Game, although this complex was not a game in the sense represented in the Whazzat Game and the Grown-up Game. This activity was a game in the sense that Hanna had fun with it, but she did not require another player, except that she had to use an adult for the original imitation. This activity combined set phrases, apparently repeated as a ritual associated with action, especially her action. The Ritual Game resembled the Whazzat Game in that it used words and linguistic patterns to accompany an action, but it differed in that it was much more varied in the patterns it employed, and in that she played it alone, although she may have been aware of her observers. Like the other games it seemed to constitute its own system. I did not hear either the words or the patterns involved in the Ritual Game appearing in any other context; Hanna had learned them as wholes and she used them as wholes, and only in the context with which she associated them.

For example there is, in the living room of Hanna's home, a chair that rocks readily, so readily that if rocked hard enough, it will go over backward, dumping a frightened Hanna on the floor. This chair, perhaps because it seemed to be playing a game with her, intrigued Hanna, so that she would frequently try to climb into it, whereat her mother would say, "Careful." Soon Hanna was saying "Careful," with her mother's precise pitches and stresses, whenever she climbed into the chair. Of course she was not being careful, and she seemed to have no notion of what *careful* was intended to imply. To her, *careful* was the accompaniment of scrambling into that chair, repeated with the tones she had learned, as a sort of ritual. Similarly, when she fell down, her mother would say, "Oh-oh," going from a high to a low pitch, in the hope of suggesting that this was no more than an amusing joke, nothing that warranted weeping calculated to gain sympathy. Soon Hanna was saying "Oh-oh," with her mother's pitch and stress, whenever she fell down.

As soon as it had occurred to me that I was observing activities of some linguistic interest, I made my gestures to science by taking tapes of Hanna's speech. To distract her, and also to keep her near the mike, my wife called Hanna's attention to the revolving reels, and said, "See. They go round and round." Hanna took this up at once, saying "round and round," although she reduced it to *ronaron*, with the stress, pitch, and juncture my wife had used in saying "It goes round and round," and her suprasegmentals were accurate, however uncertain her reproduction of the phonemes. This became the family name for a tape recorder, and Hanna associated the name with the whole object. She would start pointing and shouting *ronaron* whenever I got out of the car carrying the tape machine. Clearly she did not associate *round and round* with the action of the reels, and was somewhat disturbed when the cover was taken off the machine and placed in another part of the room, since there now seemed to be two *ronarons*, and she apparently had no sure way of dealing with this phenomenon. No doubt the confusion was augmented for Hanna because the *ronaron*, a whole, a physical and indivisible whole, was also a linguistic whole, including at a minimum a referent, a sequence of phonemes, and a pitch pattern.

Meanwhile Hanna had continued her imaginery conversations in what I have called the Playing Grown-up Game, and I so name it because, although without any real proof, I conceive that this activity was direct imitation of what she supposed adults were doing. I have the impression that she associated me particularly with this game; at least she would seize upon me and we would start playing the game at once. No doubt her mother and her sisters had to endure a good bit of this sort of thing, and they probably occasionally evinced their boredom—after all, they were exposed to it much more than was I, and they did not have my academic reasons for listening to apparently meaningless chatter. By now Hanna was "talking" more volubly, I assume because she was gaining better control of her vocal mechanisms, and partly because she remembered me better; when she was younger, if I happened not to see her for a couple of weeks, she had apparently forgotten me. Her sounds were increasing somewhat, but I made no careful analysis of these sounds. Considering the excellent research which has been published on the acquisition of speech sounds, I saw little point in doing so. The complexity of her sentence structures had apparently increased, but again I have inadequate evidence to say very precisely how the patterns were developing, although one could notice that both coordination and subordination were more extensive.

What struck me was that she was now learning grammar relatively slowly, compared with the rapidity with which she had acquired it during the first twelve months of her life, when she had learned all the basic patterns. During the next six months, however, while her use of sounds increased rapidly, she seemed to be acquiring relatively few new sound patterns. She may have learned more grammar at this time than appeared, but if my conclusions are valid I must assume that she was now hearing few sentence patterns. she did not already know, that the new ones she did hear appeared so infrequently that they did not much impinge upon her and that in any event she already had most of the patterns that would have seemed to her to be any good. Any other patterns she heard were not needed in either her cries or her games. Notable, also, was the fact that although Hanna was by now beginning to link vocabulary associated with her cries with vocabulary that was growing out of the Whazzat Game and its variations, I could detect no influence of either of these upon the Ritual Game or the Playing Grown-up Game. I did not during this time hear her say anything in the Grown-up Game suggestive of the words she used as cries, as part of a ritual, or as replies in the Whazzat Game.

Shortly before Hanna was two she began fusing her various aural systems into one and associating this one system with a true understanding of language. Words from the Whazzat Game or from her cries would now occasionally appear in the Grown-up Game, usually with some hesitation. Why she hesitated I am not sure; she may have felt unsure of herself, or she may have doubted the propriety of introducing part of one game into another. In support of this last thesis I note that she was uncommonly sensitive to any adverse comment; the mildest word of rebuke would so chasten her that she would lie down on her stomach and shut out the world by hiding her face.

At about twenty months, her mother reported that Hanna had generated her first sentence, "See the flower." Personally, I doubt that she was as yet using grammar in association with words she had learned. I did not hear her doing so at this time, but I have many times heard her sisters, in a laudable attempt to promote a sense of beauty, saying "See the flower, Hanna." I suspect that this "sentence," is of a piece with "Careful," and "Oh-oh"—a ritual to be performed under certain circumstances. I was not so fortunate as to hear this locution, but I would be fairly confident that it was uttered with the pedagogical pitch patterns of Hanna's older sisters, not with the conversational patterns she used when playing the Grown-up Game.

By the time Hanna was two her "sentences" had greatly increased in number and variety, if not much in length. I suspect that most of them were still imitations of locutions she had heard, with the pitch patterns associated, "go bed now," "go pottie," "have dinner," and by now apparently the sentence patterns she had used in the Grown-up Game were coalescing with the words she had learned in her cries, since now the cries used some of the Grown-up Game patterns. Sometime during this period, the last few months before she was two, so far as I could observe, Hanna did begin to generate sentences. The grammar was very simple, and one did not always know what she meant to say. An initial sound plus a word with the interrogative pattern might be intended for "Is it yellow?" "It's yellow?" "It yellow?" "Is yellow?" or something else, but clearly she was now able to associate vocabulary and grammar as the ingredients of communication. That is, she had developed the essential concept of language.

In the subsequent months—my subject is, at this writing, somewhat more than two and a half—Hanna has grown rapidly in linguistic sophistication. By now she has a considerable vocabulary, and is addicted to observations that convulse the family. She has now ceased entirely to play the Grown-up Game—just when, we are not sure. The family, of course, was interested in her learning to talk, not in her ceasing to babble, and it is easier to notice when things start than when they stop. All the family agrees, however, that she has not played the game for some months. Her mother confirms my impression that she went on playing the game a little when she was tired or frustrated, and this indulgence continued somewhat after the time when she had played it at every opportunity. I assume she wanted to do something with adults but could not quite face the problem of using words.

Meanwhile, Hanna continued to play the Whazzat Game with zeal and growing competence. Her indentifications speeded up, and she apparently used "Whazzat" more frequently because she wanted the information than she had earlier. Now, however, she plays Whazzat less frequently, and is apparently trying to learn to read. As for her cries and her ritualistic expressions, they blended readily with the patterns used in the Grown-up Game, and if there was any marked change here I did not notice it.

Thus, by the time Hanna was two and a half she seemed to be a normally bright child uncommonly precocious in her command of language. Personally, I suspect that this precocity is rooted more in her surroundings than in her genes. She is bright, and her parents are both intelligent and literate, but neither has special interest in language. On the other hand, she grew up among people who were reading; her sisters were in school, and dutifully did their homework, and her mother returned to college when Hanna was a few months old. To Hanna, one definition of an adult must be a person who sits and turns the pages of a book, and she does this habitually.

I suspect, also, that the conditions in Hanna's home are unusually conducive to language learning, albeit they were not consciously directed to that purpose. Most of Hanna's learning was associated with love, happiness, and fun. She would cry out "Mommy" if she was in desperate need, or if she was tired and thwarted she would seek comfort by calling for her bottle, but most of what we must call elementary language learning was associated with happiness and especially with having fun. Anything that upset her—a rebuke, fear of a stranger, a sense of tension in the family—produced either a wail or silence. Except for the limited language learning associated with her cries, Hanna used the elements of language only when she was happy, and apparently especially when she could make linguistic phenomena into a game she could play.

Now we should ask ourselves how typical Hanna's linguistic experience has been and what can be inferred from it. She is certainly not an average child; her grandmother believes she is a genius, and if her grandfather is somewhat more skeptical, obviously she is more than normally intelligent. Her household is probably unusually conducive to language learning. Everyone in it is interested in education, but more important, I suspect, everyone in it is loving and kindly. She has never been shouted at or beaten or terrorized by seeing other people fight. When she must be punished she is punished only very gently and she is made to feel that everybody loves her, although she has been a little naughty. To her, I suspect, the world is an interesting place, and not more terrorizing than a strange world must be to a small child. To her also, I surmise, adults are creatures that can be expected to play with her, be interested in her, and love her. Her mother is a gentle, charming woman and her sisters are unusually good to her. Obviously, most of the hours of her day she is happy, which means that she has had much more time for language learning than would have been hers if she had been unhappy most of her days. Furthermore, she has had plenty of time to practice her language, to develop command of her tongue, to inculcate sentence patterns, since her household has tacitly agreed that she shall be heard as well as seen.

Thus, Hanna's case is, however unfortunately for the human race, not average, but we may learn from the exceptional cases as well as from the average ones, and I suspect that Hanna's case is revealing, perhaps unusually revealing. Personally, since I am more interested in pure than in applied linguistics, I surmise that we can learn something from Hanna about the nature and history of language. Here I recall that we have never been able to agree upon the origin of language; we have devised many possible origins for language, or parts of language—that it started from cries of need or fear, from imitation of natural sounds, from the rhythm of bodily movements, from the desire to have fun making noises, and the like—but none of these seems to account for all of language or to be such a good explanation that it has displanted all the others. Now, observing Hanna, I am constrained to wonder if we have failed to find the origin of language because it never had a single origin, but resulted from the coalition of various activities, each nonlinguistic or semi-linguistic in character. Of course we cannot be sure that ontogeny repeats phylogeny, that the experience of the individual reflects the experience of the race, but we do have evidence that something of this sort is true, and certainly language in Hanna developed only after she had learned sound as cries, sound as ritual, and sound as various sorts of fun. Hanna may be, among other things, a toddling explanation of the origin of language.

However that may be, the evidence would appear incontrovertible on one point: Hanna learned sentence patterns before she learned words, any words to say nothing of most words. That is, she learned grammar before she learned vocabulary; she had learned grammatical structures before she had anything but nonsense syllables with which to flesh these skeletons. She started learning grammar earlier than she started to learn words, and she learned it so much faster than vocabulary that her rate of grammatical learning soon declined, apparently because she found little more to learn. Furthermore, she seems to have learned a sense for symbol, which she could later employ in acquiring vocabulary, before she had much vocabulary to which she might apply it.

Normally, just the opposite has been assumed. Most of the studies of children's learning of syntax have started after the subjects were two years old. Apparently the assumption was that a child could not learn grammar until he had words to talk with, and this thesis seemed to gain confirmation in the fact that children learned isolated words before they could combine these words into sentences, and when the child did form sentences he formed them with the simplest grammar, even with imperfect grammar. Thus "See kitty" was likely to precede "I can see the kitty." This sequence seemed logical, also, in that grammar was conceived to be more difficult than vocabulary. Obviously, once a child has mastered most sounds and has caught the trick of handling semantic concepts he can learn vocabulary quite rapidly, whereas grammar, at least in the limited sense of usage if not in the larger sense of language structure, continues to plague youngsters for many years, particularly the socially underprivileged.

All this seems logical, but it is so only if we assume that the child is trying to learn to talk. It does not make sense if we assume that the child is having fun, trying to please his elders, or indulging his genius as a born mimic. It makes sense if we assume that the child learns his first words in grammatical context, a grammatical context that is usable in language. It does not make sense if we realize that the child learns words like *Mommy* and *kitty* in a grammatical context that is no good to him. A year old child is not in a position to demand, "Say *Jehosaphat*, Mommy." Apparently the child learns words in context, and since his first words are learned in a context he cannot himself use, he seems to learn only the words. Similarly, a child need not learn vocabulary in order to grasp the concept of symbols; that, apparently, he can generalize from his visual observations.

That is, apparently children learn pitch, stress, juncture, and the more individual voice patterns which we might call tone, along with other understandings having linguistic use, much earlier and more easily than they learn segmental phonemes and morphemes. This theory of mine seems to gain confirmation from the learning processes of animals. Anyone who has observed a cat or a dog carefully, and especially anyone who has trained such an animal observantly, must have noticed phenomena very similar to those I recorded for Hanna. A cat or a dog may learn its name and perhaps a few other words like *kitty*, *sic 'em*, and *heel*, but not many. On the other hand, the pet will learn its master's pitch and tone very precisely, and any change in these will change the command or render it meaningless. In fact, most of the words that a pet seems to learn are probably only the accompaniment of a tone pattern; a dog that has learned *heel* is likely to respond as well to *feel* or *peel* or *keel,* but will ignore the word *heel* if it is said with a diphthong, a rising inflection, or a sing-song. That is, animals as well as babies learn grammatical patterns, and they use them, as the small child does, as a means of understanding, but for whatever reason, physical or psychological, they do not use them for creative purposes.

As a sort of corollary, one can notice that Hanna learned grammar more accurately as well as earlier and more adequately than she learned vocabulary. The sentence patterns she had learned with great skill and confidence before her first birthday, and so far as I could observe she never had to revise them. On the other hand, more than a year later she was still pronouncing quite inadequately—the tape recorder has remained to this day a *ronaron* —and although she is now learning vocabulary very rapidly she has constantly to refine the uses of the words she knows. When the Christmas tree was put up and loaded with presents she called it a *happy birthday,* since she had apparently forgotten her earlier Christmases, but had more recently become aware of parties at which gifts were given and people said "Happy Birthday." Presumably she had no grasp of concepts associated with *birth, birthday,* or even with *happy.* Two days later she was no longer calling the object a *happy birthday,* and had substituted the word *tree,* a word she knew already and one for which she had associations, but she was having trouble calling it a *Christmas tree,* although she knew the word *Christmas,* and could use it in some contexts.

Certainly, Hanna's learning of language suggests something about the nature of language learning and something of our jobs as teachers of language. Apparently, happiness and playfulness are essential ingredients of language learning; fear and embarrassment mainly inhibit it. Pretty obviously, language learning can be enhanced by providing more happy homes, and if that fact seems to shift the duty of language teaching handsomely from our shoulders to those of the parents, one can observe that we may not be able to influence parents much, but that we are responsible for at least part of what happens in classrooms. If a boy hates his father or he lives in fear of being stabbed while going to school, he may not be learning much language, and we may not be able to help greatly, but at least we can make it easy for him to play games with language and we can remind ourselves that we are likely to teach John and Mary more by encouraging them to use language, and even to play with it, than by scolding them and embarrassing them because of their ineptitudes.

We might recall also that Hanna learned most of her language in some kind of context. She learned it as games, she learned it as ritual, and if she was deliberately taught language, she still learned it in context, although usually it was an erroneous context. These feats of Hanna's suggest to us what we should guess on other bases as well: that language is learned naturally in context, that it probably is learned best or at least most easily in context and in conjunction with something else, and that we should be consciously concerned with teaching incentives and means to language.

We might notice, also, that Hanna did her best language learning without help. Her parents never consciously taught her sentence patterns—in fact, I have never known a parent who did, not even the proudest or the most demanding. Such patterns as she learned from the deliberate teaching of adults may have done her more harm than good, although not much harm—Hanna saw to that. Telling her "Say *kitty*, Hanna," taught her a pattern that was useless to her, but she readily got rid of anything she considered useless. On the other hand, the adults and older children surrounded Hanna with excellent conditions for learning language; she heard adult conversation, she was talked to and listened to, and people would play games with her, any game she wanted. She was loved and kept relatively happy. Perhaps no better school of language learning could have been devised. Hanna's mother and her sisters could not have taught Hanna to speak. Probably no human being knows enough to teach another to speak, and if there are such conversant experts, certainly they do not number many average siblings, or even super-siblings, among their ranks. But Hanna did not need teaching; all she needed was a chance to learn, and when she learned she had to learn in her own way, in a way that neighboring adults could not be expected to understand, but fortunately were ready to foster, just by being nice people.

All this leads me to my moral, which is an observation current

among teachers and even among their professors, but less extensively enshrined in conduct than I could wish. It is this: We should
ask ourselves what is our business as teachers and what is not our
business. So far as Hanna was concerned no one needed to teach
her elementary sentence patterns. Given a reasonable opportunity,
she would learn them gleefully without any help. The fact that a
teacher probably could not have taught Hanna these patterns is
beside the point; there was no need to try. A teacher needed only
to put Hanna in a position to learn. That was the best teaching,
and probably the only teaching that would have been much good.
But how about Hanna at four, at six, at eight, at fourteen, at
twenty? What can we trust Hanna to do without our help at those
ages, and what should we be doing that Hanna cannot do well, or
perhaps not do at all without our help?

Here, I believe, we need to notice some peculiarities of language and of language of learning. Learning the native language
is the most important intellectual job common to all mankind, but
it differs from most other educational activities. Within limits
it is physical; learning to speak requires learning to control the
breath, the movements of the vocal cords, and especially that subtle
and very difficult complex of muscles, the tongue, but learning to
perform these actions seems not to be inherent in an infant as is
the ability to learn to walk. Such evidence as we have of children
who have grown up without human companionship suggests that
they do not naturally learn the techniques of language. On the
other hand, language learning differs from most intellectual studies
in the sense that it is mainly unconscious. All children learn to talk,
whereas no child learns chemistry or physics or even history—at
least not much of it—except consciously.

That is, language learning differs from other learning in that,
except in its very early stages, it is essentially an intellectual
activity, it is mainly learned unconsciously, apparently by imitation,
and much of it can probably be best so learned. This does not, however, mean that language cannot and should not be taught. Even
though most language learning is unconscious, learning language
well is extremely difficult, and even after we have observed that
much language learning can be ignored by the teacher because it
can be left to the imitative powers of the child, we must still recog-

nize that a very large residue of language learning must apparently be conscious, or consciously directed, and here the teacher finds his role, and a very important one it is. So far as we know, no one has ever learned to use language well without long and exacting schooling, usually self-discipline enforced by formal training.

But what should this training be? Obviously, no one needed to teach Hanna the basic sentence patterns; true, she might later need an understanding of the relationships of these patterns to become consciously aware of their uses in order to use them as a foundation from which to construct deliberately patterns she had not learned unconsciously, but the teacher need not waste Hanna's time nor society's money teaching her what she had already learned. On the other hand, Hanna did not learn complex sentence patterns, but there will come a time when she will need them, and if she is to play any important part in the modern, complex world she must learn them, both to read sophisticated prose herself and to write with the fine distinctions required by modern society.

Fortunately, Hanna loved to learn sentence patterns, but apparently she stopped learning them because she had learned all she heard, or heard very much, and hence had no new ones to imitate. But why should she not have learned the complex patterns she would later have occasion to use? Since I am no pre-school teacher, I shall not endeavor to decide how this could or should be done, but even a layman can suggest some devices worth trying. Why should not Hanna have listened to a tape on the *ronaron* which would, let us say, repeat a portion of Lincoln's Gettysburg address over and over, played of course for brief periods but at frequent intervals? Once she came to recognize the passage— which she would do very quickly if it were always repeated with identical pitch, stress, juncture, and tone—she would be delighted at every repetition of it. Soon some of the complex patterns of sophisticated speech would have been engraved deep in Hanna's conscious or unconscious mind, or whatever it is in human beings that makes language learning possible. This may not be the best way to help small children learn, but I am confident that a little experimenting and testing will produce better means of utilizing the crucial early years of a child's life, if the procedures are based upon an understanding of how small children learn language.

This same principle can be applied at other age levels, in the elementary schools, in the secondary schools, in the colleges and universities. Yet most of the English teachers I know have not seriously asked themselves what it means for their teaching that most use of the native language is learned without any of their help. What, at the level they are teaching, can they leave to the imitative and generalizing powers of the young people themselves and what must be taught by the teacher if it is ever to be learned at all, or at least if it is to be learned economically? In my own case I am sure I have learned during the past ten or fifteen years some use of language that I might have learned earlier, that I have learned slowly and arduously what I could have learned better and with ease forty or fifty years ago if my teachers had genuinely understood their jobs.

This is not to suggest, of course, that I understand their jobs, or even my own, but it is to suggest that every teacher of English should ask himself seriously at least these three questions:

1. Do I understand how language works and how it is learned?
2. What can I trust my students to learn without my help?
3. What can I do to help my students learn what they need most?

Obviously, the answers will vary in various social groups and at various grade levels, but as some evidence that I take my own admonitions seriously, I shall report briefly a little experiment I ran in connection with a course in composition for college freshmen. Having assigned a recent speech for study, I discovered that the students could not understand it, and endeavored to find out why. I soon satisfied myself that the students were lacking in vocabulary and in a working knowledge of complex sentence patterns. Trying to discover more specifically how these areas of ignorance impeded students, I assigned various paragraphs and asked my charges to summarize each paragraph in a few sentences. The following is one of the paragraphs, from Herbert Muller's *Uses of the Past*:

> Ultimately, both the glory and the tragedy of Israel sprang from the exalted, inhuman conviction that they, and they

alone, were God's chosen people. Chosen peoples are not apt to make good neighbors. Their refusal to make peace with their Greek neighbors and their Roman rulers could be high-minded and heroic, or it could be narrow-minded and perverse. Often it was plain fanaticism. The chosen people resented the tolerance and humanism of Hellenistic Civilization as fiercely as they resented its immorality and paganism. When the ruthless, able, statesmanlike Herod the Great restored the glory of Palestine, they could forgive his brutality but not his alien birth or his fondness for Greek culture. When they were exploited by their own rich, priestly aristocracy they were docile—until the aristocracy grew friendly with the Greeks. 'As has always been the case in the East,' writes Kirsopp Lake, 'the people submitted to extortion but rebelled against civilization.' And in their periodic uprisings their zealots were as brutal as their rulers, massacring thousands of Gentiles, and murdering many of their fellow-Jews who opposed their violence. In general, the people were incapable of the humble, charitable attitude implicit in the teaching of their greatest prophets. The history of Israel, like the history of Christian Europe, suggests that no nation and no sect can afford to regard itself as the elect of God.

As a result I got no answer that I, if I were Professor Muller, would have accepted as a fair summary. Here is one, and, as a matter of fact, not one of the poorer:

> The Hebrews became the great people they are today because they were the chosen people of God. Since they were the chosen people they were exalted, and they were good neighbors, and they hated immorality and paganism. They opposed violence, but they were subjected to brutal rulers. History has rewarded them because they were tolerant and humble.

I trust I need not labor the point that although this answer shows some resemblance to Muller's paragraph it comes to almost an opposite conclusion. How did this writer achieve this feat?

The first sentence of the original is rather long and has somewhat complex structure. Apparently the student could not find his way through it, but he garnered bits familiar to him like, *exalted* and *God's chosen people.* His background being what it was, he assumed that the *exalted* described *God's chosen people,* which seemed to make sense, and he did not notice that *exalted* modifies *conviction,* a concept which he probably did not understand very well, especially taken in connection with the notion that this conviction was *inhuman.* The student apparently thought that he now knew what the paragraph would say. Accordingly, he glanced through the next sentence and picked up the familiar phrase, *good neighbors,* and since to him it would be inconceivable that God's chosen people would be bad neighbors, he did not see the word *not* at all, or he ignored it as something inexplicable. Now the student encountered a series of sentences, all rather long and complicated; clearly he did not understand them, but he picked up words like *immorality* and *paganism,* along with phrases like *opposed violence* and *brutal rulers.* These seemed to fit nicely into what he assumed the paragraph said, and since he now trusted he had enough for an adequate answer, he wrote his summary.

What was the young writer doing here? He was not reading at all in the sense that he was laboriously working through Muller's sentences, finding out exactly what each one says, and then proceeding to the next sentence. Whether he was the victim of some speed-reading course, or whether a well-intentioned teacher had taught him to skim, he was picking up words he recognized and could assume were key words. He then thought, on the basis of these words, whatever he already believed or could plausibly guess. Now, one should notice that in a well-built paragraph, such as those Muller writes, every sentence is likely to rely upon a previous sentence or paragraph or some concept clarified in them. Accordingly, if a reader misunderstands one sentence, he is likely also to misunderstand the next sentence, and even if he misunderstands each sentence by only twenty percent, sentence by sentence he gets progressively farther from what the author meant to say, so that he will soon be approaching zero comprehension, a state which most of my students achieved with great celerity.

An investigation of this sort may not be entirely revealing, pedagogically. Mine, I fear, was not. It suggests that my students are not likely to progress very rapidly; they need to be familiar with more words and they need to be able to work comfortably with complex sentence patterns, and both of these skills would require long-term development. At the least, however, I felt I had some deepened insight into the source of their troubles and I thought I knew better how to invest my time with them.

That my students were typical seems to gain confirmation from all sorts of sources. The following tale may be apocryphal, or it may be at least exaggerated, but I feel confident it is revealing. I use it in the form printed by Bennett Cerf in his column "Try and Stop Me."

> To prove how inaccurately people listen, or read, Pollster George Gallup tells of a Congressman who chided the Department of Agriculture for the trashy, useless pamphlets it publishes at the people's expense. "Seems like you fellows print every last thing about nature," he complained, "but the love life of a frog!"
>
> Promptly six letters arrived in the next two days asking for copies of "The Love Life of a Frog." Others followed in such profusion, the Department felt obliged to state in a circular, "We do NOT print 'The Love Life of a Frog.'" The result of this procedure was such a flood of new requests that the Secretary of Agriculture got into the act personally.
>
> "Confound it!" he thundered on a nation-wide program, "This Department never has printed 'The Love Life of a Frog,' and we never even want to hear about 'The Love Life of a Frog' again!"
>
> The next day there were over four hundred requests in the Department's mail.

Now we should remind ourselves that the people who ordered copies of this nonexistent study of the erotic vagaries of *Rana pipiense* had mostly been through our classes, many of our classes. Obviously, they cannot or do not read. What should we have taught them that we did not? I fear I do not know the answer, but I am confident we shall come closer to appropriate answers than we often do now if, when we ask ourselves what our business is, we will take account of the nature of language and of language learning.

--⧉ 13. ⧉--

Goldilocks and
the Three or More Rhetorics

This piece was written at the request of the University of San Francisco, which asked me to say something about rhetoric before their English Workshop in June, 1965. It was subsequently read before the San Jose State College NDEA Institute, and before the Kentucky and Greater Cleveland Councils of Teachers of English, Arizona State University, and elsewhere. It has not previously been offered for publication.

~~◄§ "Once upon a time there was a little girl, and her name was Goldilocks."

This sentence, or another much like it, is known to most children who mature in the English speaking tradition. According to handbooks of composition, this is a poor sentence, about as bad as it could be, granted that it does not defy the known grammatical principles or offend current usage. A modern writer addressing adults might start with two words, *little Goldilocks*, and would expect to include the concept of time within his verb, and would have said almost everything of importance in this fourteen-word sentence.

I submit to you, however, that this sentence is built along sound rhetorical lines, but the rhetoric is that of children. The sentence begins with a cliché, *Once upon a time*, but children love clichés, they need clichés. Children need protection and stability, some shield to fend the terrors of the unknown. They are born with the physical power to grasp, and they cling to mommy, the best protection they know against such dangers as they can conceive. A cliché is to language what mommy is to a bewildered, frightened child; in a world of grownup words and constructions, it is something to cling to, and it promises the child a story, a chance to live in a world better than the one he knows. Furthermore, the cliché in question is simple and charming, *Once upon a time*, a rhythm to be chanted.

Similarly, this sentence relies upon childish constructions. The simplest sort of grammar in English is the grammar of a single word, *ouch!*, *yes*, *mama*, but the Goldilocks sentence, if it works through grammar more sophisticated than that of one word standing alone, is not much more sophisticated. We now have reason to believe that children learn the simpler sentence patterns before they learn words, at least some kernel sentences or SVC patterns,

114

or at the latest, before they have learned many words, and the Goldilocks sequence employs a sentence combination in its simplest possible form. Aside from the opening cliché, we have a noun cluster, *a little girl,* with the SVC pattern completed in the most elementary way, with the expletive and the verb *to be, there was.* Next we have simple-minded use of coordination, *and her name was Goldilocks,* a secondary concept which cries out for subordination, except that this sentence is intended for children, and the childish mind loves undifferentiated coordination. Likewise the construction in this clause approaches the expletive in its simplicity, equated nouns linked with a copula, *name was Goldilocks,* and words occupy the most usual places; nothing intervenes within the SVC pattern, nor is there inversion or other literary artifice that might impede the readiest grasping of a childish concept. As for the diction of the sentence, it is also suited to untutored minds. Except for the name, *Goldilocks,* all are words of one or two syllables, all among the first few hundred words a child is likely to learn.

In short, if we are prepared to define rhetoric as the skillful use of the language, granted the purpose of the speaker or writer, the nature of the material to be treated, and the audience to be addressed, then the Goldilocks sentence, however naive it may appear to a mind intellectually adult, represents good rhetoric. At the same time, however, we must recognize that another sentence, penned for a different purpose and for a different audience, could also reveal good rhetoric, that if there is a rhetoric for children there must be at least one other rhetoric, a rhetoric for adults. Once we have acknowledged so much, that modern American English employs no one all-embracing rhetoric, we must admit more questions: How many rhetorics are there? What are these rhetorics? If we are teaching mainly one rhetoric to students, are we teaching the right one? I suspect that these questions have been too little asked, that they will be asked more, and asked more seriously, in the near future than they have been asked in the past. In fact I suspect that we are on the brink of a revolution. A quarter of a century ago we were moving into a revolution in our thinking about language and the teaching of language. I believe we are today moving into a comparable revolution in rhetoric, except that the new rhetorical thinking may be even more potent for the teaching of composition than was the new grammatical thinking, for the obvious reason that, in sophisticated writing, rhetoric determines more creative and editorial decisions than does grammar.

As I have implied, recent years have witnessed many contributions to rhetorical thinking including some awareness either that there is more than one rhetoric or that the word *rhetoric* can subsume more than one sort of activity. Of course it does not matter how we use the term, so long as we understand what we mean by it. Apparently Wayne Booth is using it in one way when he writes *A Rhetoric of Fiction* and Leo Rokas is using it in the other when he discusses *The Modes of Rhetoric,* as is my colleague, Robert M. Gorrell when he pens "Not by Nature: Approaches to Rhetoric." Meanwhile, the fact that Dean Daniel Fogarty publishes *Roots for a New Rhetoric* suggests that the new should differ from the old, and if Francis Christensen describes a generative rhetoric he is certainly implying that there must be another rhetoric, or another sort of rhetoric, which is not generative. Some other writers are aware that rhetoric cannot be entirely monolithic, [since this paper was written, Walker Gibson has characterized three sorts of American writing as *Tough, Sweet & Stuffy*], but even an untrammelled thinker like I. A. Richards can entitle a volume *The Philosophy of Rhetoric,* as though there could be only one rhetoric and it could have only one philosophy. Most writers on the subject seem to have tacitly accepted such assumptions.

To understand the various attitudes, we should perhaps consider the problem historically. What is our conventional rhetorical statement, and whence did it come? Superficially the answer is easy; it sprang up as do-it-yourself instructions for self-defense attorneys, and was systematized by people like Aristotle, whose *Rhetoric* was and still is a basic document. It seems that a Classical tyrant, one Thrasybulus, was uncommonly apt in appropriating other people's property, and when he was at length overthrown, the courts were flooded with cases brought by appellants endeavoring to recover their former possessions. The established practitioners being unequal to this rush of suits, schools sprang up to instruct the litigants in conducting their own cases. Significantly, these cases had their own characteristics; they were not well supported in recorded fact, since, as in many early societies relatively innocent of writing materials or even of writing ability, records of title and of real estate transactions were inadequate. Thus the early rhetorical method, while it did not neglect *inventio*—what we might call development with evidence—tended to rely on the doctrine of probability and to stress argument. Standard procedure to convince the court seems to have required a speech composed of four or five parts, depending upon what you count as a part, including an introduction or proem, a narration or invention composed of such evidence as was available, the arguments pro and con, and the peroration or conclusion. With variations in terminology, subdivisions, additions, or omissions, these parts of a composition continued to provide the basis for the art of the *rhetor,* or orator, and can still be observed in rhetorical statements today. Naturally, what passed under the term *rhetoric* was not one thing. Because using language to deceive, "to make the poorer seem the better reason," can be a profitable activity, rhetoric developed the connotation implied in the phrase "mere rhetoric" or skillful use of language for windy purposes. At the other extreme, some exponents of rhetoric thought of it as the epitome of what we associate with the liberal arts, the cultivation of the whole man, one who, under the influence of rhetoric, would become public spirited, devout, and learned.

The pattern was perhaps established by Isocrates and described by Aristotle, whose survey contrasts rhetoric and dialectic. For him, dialectic (discussion or argument), was the means of ascertaining truth, the equivalent of modern research procedures except that the Greeks assumed that truth is determined by refining one's thinking about it rather than by seeking it. Once the truth had been ascertained, rhetoric was the means by which it was promulgated, the instrument through which the hearers—whether the judge in court, the senators in session, or the unlettered many—could understand it, accept it, and act upon it. Thus, as a modern writer has put it, "there is no honest rhetoric without preceding dialectic." Despite the variation in what was covered under the hospitable blanket term, *rhetoric,* all uses of the study and practice—for rhetoric could be either or both—were concerned with the oral use of language and most of them were directed toward the persuasion of the hearers, particularly toward the moving of hearers to action. As to written language, Aristotle noted that it had little use in rhetoric except to serve as notes to prompt the memory. Even when speeches were written, they were written to be memorized and delivered. In fact, Isocrates and many other teachers of rhetoric included among the main divisions of the study effective delivery and devices for committing speeches to memory. A *rhetor* could commit no greater blunder than forgetting his speech, which some of them did, thus becoming speechless in at least two senses.

In the Middle Ages the Church embraced rhetoric. Augustine was a rhetorician before he became a convert and a bishop, and he was among those who adapted the pagan practices of persuasion to the Christian *artes praedicantium,* the art of preaching. At the same time rhetoric had some development, although not much, as a medium of writing. It was used as a formalized device for inditing letters, official princely and governmental letters, and Chaucer's poor scholar could probably have replaced his threadbare coat except that he

Ne was so worldly for to have offyce.

On the Canterbury pilgrimage he was warned to lock his colors of rhetoric in his closet, that the language in which men write to kings would be inappropriate for his audience. Thus even the use of rhetoric for formal epistles was not much more than the recording of what would ideally have been an oral address, adorned with the aureate figures thought fitting for regal ears.

From the middle of the sixteenth century the writing of rhetoric became a lively hack job in England. The study of speech had been pruned of some such excrescences as the means of committing a speech to memory, but it continued to reflect the form of a Latin oration and to perpetuate the elaborate panoply of figures of speech which ornamented classical oratory. Works like Henry Peacham's *The Gardeyn of Eloquence, Conteyning the Figures of Grammar and Rhetorick,* 1577, were likely to contain more than a hundred figures of speech, designated by names like *merismus, orismus,* and *sinathrismus,* so that for the schoolboy the study of his native language could become largely the memorizing and defining of such terms, with examples.

Thus those modern students who think of rhetoric as the way to prepare and deliver a public speech, who return to Aristotle as the fountain of their learning and the bounds of their practice, have historical reasons for this restricted use of the term and this restricted definition of their activity. A *rhetor* was an orator, and rhetoric was what he studied and did. This history can, however, be observed in another light. Aristotle described the oral use of language because, in effect, this was the only use Greeks had for it. Men could write, of course, and some could read, but writing was a rare skill and reading but little practiced. The world was as yet untroubled by mass media, nor was it aware that words could be disseminated to large numbers of people except by public oratory. When Aristotle considered the uses of oral language he was in effect studying the use of language in composition; he did not consider written composition because there was little writing to consider. He is, himself, a case in point; he was the Hellenic equivalent of a college professor, and what we call his works seem mainly to be his lecture notes, somewhat amplified by his students. Thus when Aristotle considered the most refined use of prose, he found it to be mainly comprised within oral persuasion. If we were now to ask the same questions, what is good prose used for, we should arrive at a different answer, and we should probably assume that a prose having different uses should also have different qualities.

When the problem is so phrased, almost anyone conversant with what has happened in recent grammatical thinking will be struck by an analogy, possibly an instructive analogy, with the role of Classical grammar in the writing of English grammar. As is now quite clear, early English grammarians assumed that grammar is essentially one thing, wherever it occurs, and that since the Latin and Greek languages were accepted as the best possible human speech, the grammatical descriptions of those languages would provide the best grammatical statement. To write a grammar of English, one had only to apply the Latin and Greek descriptions to the local speech. This was done; the resulting grammar books were not very satisfactory, but inadequacies were explained on the assumption that English was an inferior language, and hence could not be expected to participate much in the purest grammar. How fallacious all this was did not appear until we learned more about grammar, until we could see that Classical grammatical statements were not universal, that they were at best analyses of particular grammars, of grammars so different from the grammar of modern English that the description of either could not be expected to work well for the other. Now we have to ask whether Classical Greek and Latin rhetoric is to be relied upon as an approach to one universal rhetoric equally applicable to Modern English, or whether it may not be the rhetoric appropriate for a given language at a given time and place, but not necessarily adequate for another language at another time and place, namely modern American English.

We might ask ourselves how modern American prose differs from Classical Greek prose. Fundamentally, it differs because the cultures differ. Modern Americans place only limited reliance on arguing as a means of determining truth. They doubt that an action should inevitably be directed by the powers of oral suasion. We believe in finding truth by seeking it, by developing techniques and devices with which to find it; we could not have argued ourselves to the Moon or to a higher standard of living. Even when we hope to persuade, we expect to do so mainly by informing, by disseminating discovered truth, confident that truth, known and disseminated, will triumph. Every four years we are subject to a flood of persuasive oratory, to rhetoric in the old sense. Many voters are soon weary of it, and wish that campaigns were restricted by law. The fact is that much of the most serious communication in the United States today is written, and not mainly calculated to persuade. To verify this statement one has only to walk through the stacks of a library, totalling the volumes that are mainly persuasive in intent and method and those that are not. The total of the books that can be described by the Greek definition of rhetoric will be relatively few. Even the oral use of the language is not mainly persuasive, as anyone can prove to himself by listening to conversations, broadcasts, conferences, or anything else. Persuasion is still a class of discourse, but, outside of advertising, a minor class.

Modern American use of language differs not only in purpose. The speaker is likely to be different; many a modern author speaks or writes because he knows, not because he can brandish the rhetorical arts. John Dewey was perhaps the dullest classroom performer I have ever heard; he seemed bored with what he was saying, but everyone else wes excited. Einstein has been listened to, but not because of his figures of speech. Men like I. A. Richards and George Lyman Kittredge may be masters of the use of the English language, but they are heard mainly because they have commanded such vast reaches of learning, and have used it to think with. Others like Wehrner von Braun may have difficulty using English, but every word they pen or utter is snatched from them.

Similarly, the audience is different; broader in space and in culture, and deeper in time. Demosthenes knew that his words would not carry beyond the range of his voice, and would die with their echo. Most Greeks never heard him. A modern newspaper must be written so that every person in the community can read it, and most of them will. A writer of English knows that his book may be read in any country in the world, and that if it is at all popular, or if it is important though specialized, it will be read on all continents. Authors have to be careful not to "date" their works; books are read for years, for decades, even for centuries after they are written.

Even in the lesser units of composition, modern American English differs from Classical Greek. Professor Francis Christensen has pointed out the prevalence, I believe rightly, of what he calls the cumulative sentence in modern American prose, and has contrasted it with the periodic sentence. The periodic sentence, of course, was unusually appropriate to a Latinate grammar and to formal, oral addresses; the cumulative sentence is much better adapted to a language having an analytic grammar, and to written composition, particularly to written composition dealing with large bodies of factual material. We might notice, also, that the modern English sentence works mainly by the position of the words and by signals indicative of relationship. Classical Latin and Greek used such devices but seldom as grammar and since users of Classical Languages could place key words like the subject and verb in almost any desirable position, *rhetors* could produce remarkable turns of phrase for emphasis or variety, and they could ornament their prose with figurative tricks impossible in English. On the other hand, ornate prose is now out of fashion, and many of us find qualities in English sentence structure which we miss in Latin, a flexibility in subordination and an aptitude for concrete detail that is suitable to a complex society and a specialized technology.

Similarly modern English, perhaps particularly modern American English, uses words differently than did the Classical tongues. Since Latin and Greek relied extensively upon inflection, that is, upon change in the form of a word to reveal its grammatical use, the reader usually knows how a Latin or Greek word is working in a sentence, regardless of the other words in the same sentence. In English this is not true. The use of the word is usually vested within the word itself, or is revealed through other words. For example take a sentence that begins, "He pressed his suit with the . . ." If we now complete the sentence with the word *lady*, we have the description of a Victorian love affair, but if we complete the sentence with *iron* we are discussing an operation suited to the laundry. Furthermore, most of the words in the sentence work differently as well as mean differently, depending upon how the sentence is completed.

That is, from the largest to the smallest aspects of composition, we have no reason to suppose that a statement adequate for Greek would be adequate for modern American English. Greece was a little country, not long out of barbarism; Athens was a small town, and most Greeks were slaves, farmers, or fishermen. The United States today has developed the most complex social and economic structure that history records, and whatever it is, it is growing daily more so. This may be no good thing; it may be a very bad one, but it gives us no reason to suppose that we can import from a relatively rural community like Greece an appropriate description of the way to use our language. This impracticality is accentuated, furthermore, by the fact that the two languages are fundamentally different, and that in the use of language we cannot well ignore the nature of the language we are using.

What answers would we get if we were to ask ourselves how

we can best use modern English, whether we call this study of the studied use of language composition, Freshman English, or "the new rhetoric"? On the whole, in recent years, two sorts of people have ventured upon such questions. A few highly intelligent, deeply philosophic persons have asked questions about the use of language, people like I. A. Richards and Kenneth Burke. Their speculations have been interesting, but are as yet inconclusive. The second sort of person has been mainly concerned with teaching. Some of these have assumed that rhetoric is about what Aristotle described and have tried to find use for it in courses, an attempt in which they have had some success. Others, apparently assuming that *rhetoric* is only a fancier name for composition, have asked what a young person needs to know in order to write correctly, and through what paces he should be put so that his writing will improve. Some of these people have produced very good answers; the level of composition textbooks has risen remarkably in this country in the past half century, but most of the textbook writers have written, I should say, either without much benefit of Classical rhetoric, or too much in its shadow. Classical rhetoric at its best was not picayune; it attacked the most fundamental problems. On the other hand, some modern textbook makers have been less concerned with helping people to write than with scolding them for mistakes. Others have assumed the mantle of amplitude bequeathed by the rhetoricians, but they have tended not to escape from the mantle.

For example, many have assumed that the four forms of discourse are narration, description, argumentation, and exposition. I am not sure what the modern forms of discourse may be, but I am sure they are not naturally and adequately denominated as these four. The technique of the novel differs from the technique of the short story, and both are so different from what the historian or the journalist means by a narrative that surely we are here in the presence of major distinctions. A novel and a history differ in purpose, method, vocabulary, in almost everything. Thus narration is more than one thing, but we might argue that description is no form of discourse at all, but rather a method within narration or exposition, which likewise is probably not one thing. And certainly argumentation is not one thing; a roadside billboard or a singing commercial do not much resemble a lawyer's brief, although both are calculated to persuade.

Thus the analogy between rhetoric and grammar is perhaps instructive, at least insofar as our conventional statements have rested upon Classical materials. The Classical grammatical statement has had its uses; it recognized the sentence, the clause, the predicate, the phrase, and a good many concepts which, with revisions, have survived all attacks. On the other hand, the universality of the Classical grammatical statement interfered with fresh approaches; adapting Latin grammar to vernacular languages required bold thinking, and most of the older grammarians were not bold enough. Even the philologists, who recognized that every grammar must be derived from its own language, managed to construct grammars for English which were remarkably like those for Latin. Similarly, the Classical rhetorical statement is not without its pertinence; compositions do have beginnings, middles, and endings, or at least many do. Telling a story does differ in notable ways from explaining a principle, and a skillful writer can do tricks with language that at once delight readers and clarify meaning, but writers on language who have endeavored to import into English the virtues of Classical rhetoric have often imported too blindly and questioned too little. Seeing that Classical rhetoric has virtues they did not notice how great may be its limitations. Even Richards, whom I have praised above, wrote as follows: "Rhetoric, I shall urge, should be a study of misunderstanding and its remedies." This observation comes from one of his earlier writings, and I suspect that he would now be more likely to say, "Rhetoric should be the study of understanding, and how to promote it." If so this is only further evidence that we need new rhetorical statements in America, and that we are in the process of forming them.

What is the rhetoric of modern American English? What should our rhetorical statement be? I confess I do not know, and I do not know anyone who does. We are making progress, but more progress is to be made. I have suggested above that we shall probably need to develop more than one rhetorical statement, and I should add that these are likely to differ so sharply from one another that, in many details, they may be contradictory. Of course even Classical rhetoric showed some variety; the rhetoric of a pleader before a court differed somewhat from the rhetoric of a senator addressing other senators, but perhaps not much. After all, rhetorical statements concerned oral composition looking toward delivery; rhetoric was persuasive in intent, and it tended to be formally prescribed. Prose fiction did not exist; the novel had not yet been invented. The great need for knowing had not yet arisen; investigative and expository prose, using written words for both creation and preservation, was as yet so little the answer to a felt need that thinkers like Aristotle ignored it. We are no longer limited, however, as were the Greeks, and I suspect we shall find the need for more than one rhetorical approach.

As this hour draws to a close, some of you may be recalling the ancient and dishonorable device which we might call flunker's gambit, by which students distract the teacher's attention to avoid embarrassing questions. You may well be aware that I have consumed so much of my time—and yours—with histories and analogies, that I have now but little freedom to consider the main questions, what are the modern American rhetorical statements, or what should they be? If you have entertained this notion, you have reason. I should not now have time to answer such questions even if I knew the answers, which I freely confess I do not. Personally, I have done too little thinking and too little searching; and although others have done more, the findings I might report to you leave major questions unresolved, sometimes unasked. I can offer only preliminary guesses.

I should divide modern American writing into two sorts, and perhaps for no better reason than to coin a rhetorical phrase, I shall call them *the rhetoric of expression* and *the rhetoric of impression,* the first governed by the needs of the author, the second by the needs of the audience. The first would include what is often called *belles lettres,* writing in which the author believes he has something important to say, something that comes out of him as a human being and receives its impress from him as a literary artist. It would include poetry, the personal essay—which would have strong affinities with some sorts of the rhetoric of impression—and creative fiction, which in turn would have various subdivisions, of which the most obvious might be the rhetoric of the novel and the rhetoric of the short story. These categories will not be rigid, of course; in anything as fluid as writing no categories can be absolute. Rhetorical statements can be no better than revelational, never prescriptive, and they may be expected to shift and grow—after all, we are presumably not the ultimate human beings. I am told, for example, that the novel as it is developing in Europe has little to do with telling a story, very much as the novel, as it altered under the impact of James Joyce, may have little to do with chronology. However that may be, I shall say little more this morning about the rhetoric of expression since it has already been widely and intelligently discussed under such headings as literary criticism, the art of fiction, poetry, and the like, if not much in connection with the word *rhetoric*.

Now to the rhetoric of impression. The main line of subdivision here may be that between the rhetoric of mass media and the rhetoric of informed discussion. The former includes, of course, the rhetoric of radio and television, the rhetoric of news reporting and the somewhat different rhetoric of newspaper entertainment and discussion. Even in the newest of the mass media, conventions are crystallizing; for example, no self-respecting newscaster reporting from a special assignment can close without something like the following signoff, "With the monsoon season beginning, and the Viet Cong dug in ever more solidly in the jungles, fighting here can be expected to grow worse before it grows better, if it ever does. This is Johnny Walkie-Talkie, reporting for XYZ Television in Saigon." The rhetoric of mass media would presumably include much commercial fiction, however disseminated, although the techniques of commercial short stories and drama show some overlapping with similar genre within *belles lettres*. Advertising relies on the mass media and takes some of its characteristics from them, while drawing also on the rhetoric of informed discussion.

The rhetoric of informed discussion, also, has its subdivisions, the most important being, I should say, the rhetoric of information and the rhetoric of investigation. In the first of these categories, someone who presumably knows endeavors to inform other persons who presumably do not know, or are less informed than he. This category includes all sorts of informed writing in nonfiction trade books, in textbooks, and in articles of a serious nature. It can, of course, include either exposition or argumentation in the conventional sense, and in most instances it would include some of each, but the style of writing has its reason for existence in that somebody needs to be informed or persuaded, and also that somebody is presumably sufficiently informed to fill this need. Naturally, much narration of a serious and informed nature would be included here —the account of a polar exploration, for example—and this subclassification would require some observations in common with fictional narrative.

Under the heading "rhetoric of informed discussion," would be included most of the content of the traditional rhetoric, that is, persuasive oratory, whether political or juridical. Even the campaign speech would be included here, since presumably the campaigner is well informed about himself, and his audience is not. Here, as elsewhere, we could distinguish divisions and subdivisions. I have been interested to observe, for example, the growth of what might be called the "those-who" approach in sentence structure. It allows politicians to attack opponents without naming them, as in "those who indulge in slur and innuendo," "those who follow the banner of opposition for opposition's sake," "those who declare they wish to debate the issues, but refuse open debate on television before the people," and many more. The cartoonist, Herblock, has coined a pleasant phrase for it, "to indulge in nonpersonalities." It allows representatives of states and nations to condemn one another while avoiding some of the consequences of excoriation, as in "those who fish in troubled waters," "those who beat their plowshares into swords," and "those who use the sacred words of liberty and democracy to mask their attempts to deprive subject peoples of liberty and democratic justice." This rhetorical stance has advantages; it permits a speaker to condemn, but prevents the accused from replying without identifying himself as one who may be guilty. It is an ancient device, but one which has flourished in an age of international and inter-party invective.

The remaining main category we might call the rhetoric of learned investigation. It includes the sort of writing that scientists address to one another, that scholars use with other scholars, and that informed speculators upon the future pen when they write on the assumption that nobody knows the answers and that probably no one can know them, but that thinking aloud may be beneficial.

To distinguish these two sorts of writing we might consider the production of almost any specialist who has addressed the general public in popularized publications and his fellow investigators in specialized journals. For example, when Franz Boas wrote *The Mind of Primitive Man* he was composing in accordance with the principles which I have called the rhetoric of informed discussion. As a student of primitive mentality he was talking intelligibly to readers who do not much understand primitive people. At the same time, this same Franz Boas was filling many pages of the *Bulletins* and *Proceedings* of the Bureau of American Ethnology, where he would never have posed before his fellow ethnologists as knowing all the answers; rather, he presented such evidence as he had, and endeavored to speculate with other investigators as to what the truth might be about such Indians as the Bella Coola and the Tlingit.

Similarly, we can observe Margaret Mead writing in one way in *Coming of Age in Samoa,* where she addresses a serious but undifferentiated audience, and in a quite different way when she publishes in a learned journal. Rachel Carson charmed millions in books like *Under The Sea Wind,* where she employs what would be conventionally called exposition and narration, revealing marine biology through the life of a mackerel, but when she addressed her fellow marine biologists I assume she never suggested that she possessed all the secrets of the sea. Similar observations could be made about thousands of others; Professor W. Nelson Francis discussed certain obscure thirteenth-century Middle English and Anglo-Norman penance manuals, and wrote quite differently for the few hundred scholars throughout the world who may be expected to have some interest in such matters, than he did when he discussed modern linguistics for the benefit of undergraduates.

What, then, should the new rhetoric be? I should say that we cannot expect to have a new rhetoric, if by a new rhetoric we expect one inclusive rhetorical statement, and if we are to talk realistic good sense about writing we shall need more than one rhetorical statement. We shall no doubt find many principles having broad application, and many of these will already have been well outlined in the Classical rhetoric that is part of our gorgeous heritage from Greek and Latin. On the other hand we shall, I am sure, find such varying rhetorical practices in various sorts of modern writing that distinctions will be worth delineating; and these will include observations not recorded by Aristotle.

For example, consider the way in which a composition starts. Aristotle and others recommended what they called a proem, an introduction. Such an admonition is no longer universally applicable. True, a skillful novelist will draft his opening with the greatest care, introducing the long lines of his plot, setting the tone of his characterizations, developing our concern for details which will later undergo symbolic growth, but he is not likely to write anything recognizable as a proem. A writer for the mass media may feel he must do something in the first few lines or the first few minutes to intrigue his audience, to keep the viewer from switching to another channel or the reader from flipping to another and seemingly more attractive page. On the other hand, if a scientist reading a paper before a meeting of his fellow specialists were to start by telling a few conventional jokes to attract his hearers' attention, the fiasco would be a scandal. His hearers would resent this intrusion upon their time, and the implication that they are not sufficiently scientific, if the speaker has anything to say, to need no titillating. That is, the speaker would be demonstrating ignorance of what I have called the rhetoric of learned investigation.

The new rhetoric must deal, also, with the smallest units of composition; for example with the sentence. Here we might observe that we have been so indifferent to our own way of writing, so blind to the necessity of founding our auctorial present on our rhetorical past that we have no book-length history of the English sentence. Mainly we have been content to assume that what was good for Cicero was good enough for us, not only good enough, but most appropriate. It may not be.

Since the English sentence relies grammatically upon the subject-verb-complement sequence as the core of what we might call the standard sentence pattern, composition must develop rhetorically along relatively few lines. Sentences can be composed with nothing but the grammatical core and with all parts in their simplest possible form: *I love you; Johnny hates English.* Such sentences have their uses. Likewise, the order of these core units can be changed for special purposes, for questions, for emphasis, and the like, and simple kernels can be compounded; but in a complex and sophisticated world that can function only with elaborately constructed discourse, economical communication usually requires patterns in which the subject-verb-complement core plays among a variety of other elements. These elements may be scattered through the sentence, allowed to fall wherever clarity and economy suggest, or they may be controlled for special effects. Two devices suggest the possibilities; a writer can make his kernel statement at once, and append modifying, restricting, and developing bits to it, or he can hold back all or part of his core predication while he marshalls his modifiers and completes the subject-verb-complement sequence as he closes his sentence.

The second, called the periodic sentence, has traditionally been the admired structure and, recalling the history of our rhetorical statement, we can readily understand why. It is tense, oratorical, dramatic. It permitted the *rhetor* to build his rhetoric with his platform fervor, holding back all but the clinching word so that his sentence rolled to a thundering climax, and it permitted him to take every advantage of a language which did not need word order for grammar, to indulge in garlands of floral rhetoric. Notice the periodic patterns in Lincoln's Gettysburg address. Lincoln was far too skillful a stylist to rely only on pure periodic structures, but he had studied the Classical orators, and he knew how to cast his most telling sentences in a generally periodic mold: "But in a larger sense we cannot dedicate—we cannot consecrate—we cannot hallow— this ground." Then, in his great terminal sentence, he contrives a tricolon within a tricolon, building to climax after climax in what are essentially periodic structures:

> It is rather for us to be here dedicated to the great task remaining before us—that from these honored dead we take increased devotion to that cause for which they gave the last full measure of devotion—that we here highly resolve that these dead shall not have died in vain—that this nation, under God, shall have a new birth of freedom—and that government of the people, by the people, for the people, shall not perish from the earth.

These are monumental periods, and granted the time, the persons, and the place, it was altogether fitting and proper, if you will allow me to parody Lincoln's words, that the President of the United States, standing under the shadow of war and above the graves of heroes, should do this. Most of us, however, are not presidents of the United States saddened by countless dead and striving to save a nation, and we do not spend our time dedicating military cemeteries. Appropriate as such rhetoric was to the needs of Gettysburg in 1863, it would not be fitting and proper for a scientific discussion of the smog-problem in Los Angeles in 1966. Neither would such structures be appropriate to you, as teachers, who need a rhetoric of your own, when you try to explain to Mary how to use source materials without plagiarism.

More congenial to most modern Americans, apparently, is the cumulative sentence. When I was writing this paper, I decided to illustrate this device by using James Thurber, whose prose is probably as characteristic of good American writing as anything one could choose. To parallel the Gettysburg sentence as nearly as practical I turned to Thurber's biography of Harold W. Ross, founding editor of the *New Yorker*, and opened it at the first page. Inevitably, my eye hit the following sentence, since it is Thurber's one-sentence eulogy of Ross:

> Ross is still all over the place for many of us, vitally stalking the corridors of our lives, disturbed and disturbing, fretting, stimulating, more evident in death than the living presence of ordinary men.

Here we have the pattern, the quick, simple statement at once, "Ross is still all over the place," rather like a brief topic sentence, which is then developed with details so that the whole sentence becomes almost a little paragraph. Nor is this pattern unusual with Thurber; turning the page, I noticed the following:

> I had caught glimpses of him at the theater and at the Algonquin and, like everybody else, was familiar with the mobile face that constantly changed expression, the carrying voice, the eloquent large-fingered hands that were never in repose, but kept darting this way and that to emphasize his points or running through the thatch of hair that stood

straight up until Ina Claire said she would like to take her shoes off and walk through it.

And so on. Thurber knows the use of a brief, unornamented sentence, and he can build his materials into easy periods—one suspects that he, too, has studied Classical rhetoric, and certainly he knows that minor details are often best dispatched early in a sentence—but time and again his most telling structures are cumulative. They have the easy, relaxed quality of a professional, but they do an unbelievable amount of work. They carry a staggering weight of detail, but they shoulder it nonchalantly.

In short, such sentences seem to be suited at once to the English language and to a society groaning under its load of learning. Such sentences are probably native to an analytic language, or at least to the brand of analytic grammar we find in English. At any rate one notices that they abound in *Beowulf*, that they are common in Chaucer, and that they appear consistently in many a writer like Sir Richard Steele, who resisted the Classics as he did the Establishment of his day. Sentences with structures like these seem well suited to modern America; we are the people of the complex technical age, the children of the knowledge explosion, the urbanites who must survive by complexity or not survive at all. Apparently a sentence that can take up the burden of detail and handle it nonchalantly, which can provide the greatest possible diversity in subordination, is our kind of sentence.

One could go on. Obviously, we know too little of the modern American sentence and its aptness for modern American uses. Similarly we might study the means by which, in an uncertain world, the sentient writer is able to reveal the degree of his uncertainty—a limitation which did not much trouble the Classical orator since those who try to persuade others must first persuade themselves that they have all the answers. Here and elsewhere we are likely to find that our conventional rhetorical statement will warrant both correction and amplification. In the next few years it is likely to experience both.

◦◦◦ 14. ◦◦◦

The Four Forms of Discourse, New Style

The four forms of discourse, as I conceive them, are certainly not the traditional four: narration, description, exposition, and argumentation. Actually the lecture, in spite of its title, is mainly about teaching creative writing. It was prepared at the invitation of the Idaho Council of Teachers of English, about 1965. So far as I recall it has not been published.

⟶⟩ The committee that planned this conference wanted something said about creative writing and its teaching in the schools. This was, I am sure, a good idea, and even inviting me to speak may not have been an entirely bad idea; I ought to be just about ignorant enough to say something. To make a speech a man has to know something, but if he knows very much he is likely to have sense enough not to deliver a speech. Since I started teaching nearly a half century ago, I ought to know something about it, but the more I teach and the more I discuss it the more I realize that very few people understand teaching well enough to talk much sense on the subject. Similarly, I ought to know something about creative writing; I have published two novels which I do not now recommend that anybody read, and the fact that I have written no more and no better ones should be evidence that I do not know enough about creative writing to inhibit me or anyone else. I ought to be just about incompetent enough to do the job.

Accordingly, I welcome this assignment, but before I start it seriously, I shall take a cue from that other old incompetent, Shakespeare's Polonius, hoping "by indirection [to] find directions out." First let me remind you that we have experienced a revolution in our profession, and that all of us, as students or teachers or both, have lived through it, or at least an important phase of it. English is now taught much better in this country than it was a quarter of a century ago because in that time our teaching has been rejuvenated.

As an extreme example of what the teaching of English used to be like, I recall a former colleague whom the students called the Queen of the Comma Fault, when they did not use more expressive epithets which they deemed unfit for faculty ears. Actually, they rather liked her; she was a bouncy, beaming woman, not very tall but otherwise ample, and in a grudging way the students respected her for flunking them, although they seemed to sense that there was something wrong with her pedagogy, and I am sure they were right. She had a unique and infallible device for failing everybody, at least until the end of the semester, when she would relent and pass some of the better ones. She demanded themes, and after a fashion she read them; at least she read until she found what she felt to be a misplaced comma, whereupon she dashed the offending point with red ink, inscribed a large red F on the outside of the paper, and she was done. I have never been sure whether she did more harm or more good. Certainly she made some students work, and she taught some of them to punctuate, at least by her rules. She even taught more than she professed; she was an intelligent and devoted woman, with considerable taste and judgment, who knew good prose when she saw it, and she thus helped many students in ways having to do with more than comma faults. On the other hand, she confirmed many a young person in the belief that the study of his native language is nothing but commas and that English teachers are a strange lot of cranks not very useful in a civilized society.

Fortunately, the Queen of the Comma Fault was not typical of the English teachers in her day, but she was more nearly typical than I could have wished. Many a so-called course in English relied upon a grammatical statement which described no language that has ever been used by man, along with some spelling, punctuation, and capitalization. Teachers also urged that certain words were bad, or wrong, or barbarous. Meanwhile, most of the students went on writing and speaking pretty much as they had before. Some teachers taught a little sentence structure—at least they taught against the sentence fragment, but few of them taught young people how to write sentences—and a few even taught a bit of paragraphing, but most college freshmen that I encountered in those days had no real notion of what a paragraph is, except that it begins with an indentation. Some teachers taught the four forms of discourse recognized by Greek rhetoric—exposition, argumentation, description, and narration—but since these are certainly not the four main, inclusive forms of modern American composition, we need not be much surprised if this teaching had little effect. Study after study demonstrated that the teaching of what was called *English* was having only minor impact on the ability of students to read, write, or speak, but most teachers went on telling their students that a sentence is a complete thought, that a noun is the name of a person, place or thing, all the while feeling that they were fighting the good fight.

Then came the revolution. It has, I believe, some years yet to run, and we as English teachers still have a long way to go, but much has happened in recent decades. School systems are becoming convinced—or at least some of them are—that teachers must be cultured human beings, not robots with a method. Colleges and universities are doing a rather better job of preparing teachers; meanwhile, salaries are rising, so that increasingly men go into teaching, and more women look upon teaching as a dedicated profession, as something other than a respectable means of paying the bills until they are saved by matrimony. And most important from out point of view, more and more teachers of English have come to believe that the teaching of the use of the native language can be a challengingly important assignment, that the use of the language can be taught, and they are beginning to find out how to do it. By putting the teaching of creative writing on the agenda this morning I take it your committee is suggesting that here we have one of the areas in which many of our teachers are as yet too inexperienced, in which curricula tend to be inadequate, in which the revolution has lagged a bit.

I should say they are right, but before I broach my subject let me review the whole area of student writing. Commonly, I notice that students are asked to write any of four sorts of compositions, which I shall distinguish as What I Did, What I Think, What I Know, and What I Feel. They all have their uses, although some have pretty limited uses. The simplest is the What-I-Did theme, of which My Summer Vacation may be typical. I assume that topics like this are assigned because teachers are either uninspired or desperate, and faced with a roomful of wriggling and not very literate youth, I cannot blame them for being both. They assign a topic of this sort because they are too busy or too mentally weary to prepare a good subject, or they assign it because it is the easiest subject they can think of, and they are happy if they can induce their little dullards, delinquents, and potential dropouts to say anything about anything. For such purposes a theme on My First Dance or An Exciting Basketball Game may have some use, but it seldom stimulates significant prose.

The second sort of writing, the What-I-Think theme, is today perhaps the most widely admired sort in the secondary schools, at least if my students are typical. Young people are encouraged to record what they think about Skiing as a Sport, about The War in Vietnam, about The Problem of Juvenile Delinquency, and Will the Two-Party System Survive? This sort of writing has some use; young people are encouraged to examine themselves, to deal with ideas on any level they can reach, and to grow up to ideas with which they may as yet not be familiar. This is to the good or at least it can be, but the difficulty is that to think one must have information to think with, and most young people have very little. Thus, when they are asked what they think they do not think at all; they just air their prejudices, and in the process of airing them they do little but confirm them, however ill founded they may be. Thus, the theme on What I Think, unless it is carefully handled, is likely to encourage neither thinking nor sound writing, since, in order to use language well a writer must have something to say, and youngsters asked to produce a What-I-Think theme are likely to have little to say. Thus they get training in using words to say nothing, an unfortunate propensity in which they need no encouragement.

As a college teacher this has frequently been borne in upon me. I have assigned an essay, or some other piece of writing to be read, and I have asked the students to record in their own words what the author says. They are baffled. Apparently they have never been asked to do this before, and my words mean nothing to them. "Do you want me to tell what I think," they ask hopefully. I reply that I have no doubt they have beautiful thoughts, and that on another occasion I shall be glad to know about them, but just for now I do not want to know what they think; I want to know what the author thinks. They make no sense of this; they flop and flounder, and find they cannot read the passage in any real sense, that they cannot bring themselves to ask seriously what the author says. They want to say they agree or do not agree, without first finding out what they are agreeing with. Eventually they learn, and then they find that trying to record information, especially rather complex information, can be useful and can even be fun. For us as teachers, however, I believe the moral is that we should be careful how we assign What-I-Think themes until we have assigned What-I-Know themes, so that the student has something to think with.

In the secondary schools some of the best writing of the What-I-Know sort is done for the school paper. If a youngster can recognize that a committee meeting is a group of people deliberating, that the actuality of people saying things is a sort of fact, and that these facts can be built into an account of a meeting, he will have learned a great deal about writing that he probably did not know before. I find that most college students cannot do this, and apparently most high school students do not do it. I might add that on the college level this sort of informed, objective writing has been greatly promoted by the casebooks of source materials which have been widely used during recent years, but such books have not as yet much found their way into the secondary schools.

I now come to my ostensible subject, the fourth kind of writing assignment, the What-I-Feel theme, that is, creative writing. Here we are faced at once with the fact that creative writing, to be any good as writing, must be extremely good indeed, something quite beyond the powers of our young scribblers. Furthermore, as direct job training nothing could be much less appropriate than creative writing. There always have been, and there probably always will be ten, or fifty, or a hundred, or some astronomical number of people who want to be creative writers for every one who has enough genius so that there is any financial, professional, or artistic reason for his trying to become one. Ordinary creative writers are not in demand, and even good ones are not paid much. Why, then, should we teach creative writing?

Here I am reminded of a little incident on a neighboring campus. The School of Business was revamping its curriculum; some of the staff wanted more courses in accounting, some wanted more in economics, and some wanted more in office management. Accordingly, they imported an expert to give them advice, and the various sides worked on the expert to encourage him to support their courses. He confounded them all by recommending a course in creative writing. Asked to explain this seemingly insane notion, he pointed out that the ability business men need most is command of the native language, and that a student learns more about the use of language by trying to do creative writing than in any other way. Of course the School of Business did not take his advice; they require no course in creative writing, and I fancy they have increased the courses offered by all three of the warring factions, but I still suspect that the visiting expert had a point. He seems to have understood that the felt need to get the truth on paper, to crystallize a sort of reality that has become at once manifest and one's own, the job of wrestling with language to make it say as much as possible, that all this is one of the most seminal experiences the human mind and maturing consciousness can undergo.

How should one teach creative writing? I am not sure I know, but I can tell you something of how not to teach it, and here I am reminded of an experience I had when I was on the faculty at what is now Idaho State University in Pocatello. Two bus loads of students arrived one evening and were granted permission to use university facilities. I was waited upon by the young man running the project. It seems he was employed at a little southern college and he had sold the administration on the idea of a roving college; the buses would take the students from one tourist spot to another, and he would lecture at them. He had come to see me because he had to lecture the next morning, and he did not know what to say. He told me he had contracted to give a course in creative writing because he thought that would be pretty easy, and he had brought along a book from the college library. Every night he would read a chapter in the book and summarize it the next morning as his lecture, but he had not had time to finish the chapter for tomorrow, and he could not understand it anyhow. It was about *ver-i-sim-il-i-tude*—he had to look up the word in the book and sound it out—and he wanted to know if he was pronouncing it correctly. I asked him if he had ever made a practice of doing creative writing, and he looked at me as though I had asked him if he had ever made a practice of shooting his grandmothers. I am fairly sure that his is not the way to teach creative writing.

But how should one teach it? I hope my question to the itinerant pedagogue contains the germ of the answer. At least I meant it to suggest the answer. I assume one of the sound pedagogical principles is this, that whoever tries to teach another to do something should first try to do it himself. No teacher of arithmetic would try to teach long division without first trying to do long division. Doing long division is relatively simple compared with writing a poem, but for some reason a teacher of English will ask students to write a poem without first trying to write one.

This is not at all to say that to be a good teacher of creative writing the instructor must himself be a good creative writer. Teaching is a profession, and to teach successfully one must first of all be a teacher. Not every good creative writer is, or ever could be a good teacher, particularly for relatively young people. Hemingway, although he was a superb novelist, might not have been a good sixth-grade teacher of anything, even writing novels. I doubt that he would have been. Faulkner was an excellent novelist, and I am told he raised good mules and was a competent Boy Scout leader; he lectured brilliantly to college students, but he might or might not have been good with eight-year olds. I suspect that Robert Frost would have been a superb teacher at every level, but I doubt that Edna St. Vincent Millay would have been a good teacher at any level, which is, of course, no criticism of her as a poet. But a good teacher of creative writing must at least have tried to do creative writing, even though the results are bad creative art.

That is, to teach creative writing an instructor need not be a Saul Bellow or a Eugene O'Neill, but he must have had first-hand experience with the tantalizing fascination of a blank sheet of white paper. He should read creative writing; he should read it because he loves it and because he feels the urge to study it. I am sure you have all had courses in literature, and this is to the good, but I should say that, unsupported by a teacher's self-generated zeal, courses are not enough. I should be glad to be proved wrong, but I would fear there would not be one in ten in my audience who today owns one volume of poetry which he was not forced to buy, which he had heard about or read about and went and bought, just because he wanted to own it, to live with it, and genuinely to possess its contents. I fear that any teacher of creative writing who does not himself love creative writing will not do a very good job.

Third, I assume that a teacher of creative writing should study it seriously. No good teacher of physics would feel he could teach physics well unless he had studied seriously the nature of matter.

On the other hand, I fear that many teachers of English do not, at least once a year, make a serious study of one poem, one short story, one play, or one novel. I think they should, and fortunately they can now get good help. We have a large and growing body of literary explication, of modern critical appraisal. Anyone who wants help in critical understanding these days can get it, and I should say that no teacher should expect to inspire others to write until he has himself made some serious study of writing.

As to the teaching of creative writing, no doubt some methods are better than others. I noticed last summer that my colleague, Walter Van Tilburg Clark—who happens to be a superb teacher as well as a fine novelist—was having uncommon success with both secondary and elementary teachers, getting them to write haikus. Other teachers have done well with ballads, even with sonnets. One obvious good trick is to read half a story to a class, and ask the students to finish it. Another is to give them a plot, say one of the tales in the Old Testament, and ask them to write it with modern characters. I have had some success by outlining a simple plot and asking students to write two versions, imitating two different authors, say James Fennimore Cooper and J. D. Salinger, or whomever the students know. But on the whole I am suggesting that methodology is not what is lacking.

I lately participated in the unpleasant necessity of failing a candidate for an advanced degree in teaching. I was glad to find that he taught creative writing, and I asked him for the name of a good book he had read recently that nobody had told him to read for a course. He looked at me, bewildered, and said, "A book?" "Yes," I said, "a book. You know, the sort of oblong things." "Now that is a poser," he acknowledged with a grudging sort of respect. He laughed a little and tried to think. He could not remember ever having read a book, just to read a book. So I asked him if he knew the names of any modern writers. He could not remember one, nor could he recognize names that I volunteered. We had to fail the young man, regrettably, for he seemed to be a bright fellow, not because he did not know enough about methodology, but because he was too ignorant. He did not know the subject he was professing to teach. I fear he is not alone. I suspect that many teachers do not teach creative writing because they are aware that they do not understand creative writing. For this restraint I respect them, even though I regret the omission. I suspect that creative writing can be successfully taught only by those who know and love literature, but fortunately, some who do not now love it could learn if they were to expose themselves to it. And I believe I can assure you—and many, I am happy to say, will need no assurance—that creative writing can provide your students with some of their most rewarding experiences, and it can offer you some of the most satisfying teaching that, as a professional person, you have ever enjoyed.

-◄ 15. ►-

More About
Creative Writing

This piece was written for delivery at the 1957 meeting of the National Council of Teachers of English in Minneapolis, where it was to have been a rejoinder to the principal paper of the session. Unfortunately, the sharpness of any possible clash was blunted by the principal speaker's having written his address too late for me to make much use of it. Accordingly, in printing part of my remarks I have cashiered some local dialogue.

⸺⸱⸱⸱ Creative writers, so far as I have been able to observe them, differ rather sharply as to the propriety of teaching their craft. Some, like Wallace Stegner, Walter Van Tilburg Clark, and Paul Engle believe in teaching all sorts of composition from Shapiro-like verse on down, and earn a living partly by this teaching; others believe that creative writing cannot or should not be taught, and that trying to to teach it is either ill-advised or downright vicious. I have never had the pleasure of discussing teaching with our principal speaker, but I do recall a discussion with another writer, markedly different from him; she was female and somewhat enlivened with martinis. Whether either of these individualities bore on the conversation I cannot say, but when I was introduced as a professor in the local institution and a teacher of creative writing she announced, promptly and emphatically, that creative writing could not be taught. She did not add audibly, although I thought I detected in the determined manner in which she sipped her martini that she considered adding, that only a fool or a scamp would ever attempt to teach it.

I did not do well in the subsequent exchange. I soon discovered that my assailant—for such she rapidly became—possessed most of the available arsenal. She had just published a novel which was receiving at least some critical attention, and I had just published a novel which was receiving no attention at all. She seemed to feel that she was thereby an authority on whether the writing of novels could or could not be taught and that I was thereby an ignoramus. I suspected a fallacy here, that just because she had written one successful novel she could *ipso facto* infallibly tell everybody else how they could or could not learn to write any sort of creative composition, but the detection of fallacies in an argument is no good unless you can make your opponent see that she is fallacious, and I, being several martinis behind her, was inhibited by a

144

masculine reticence. Accordingly, whether I was downed by her eloquence or my sobriety, I shall remark only that had her attack been as devastating as it purported to be, there would exist by now no such activity as the teaching of creative writing.

If I fared but ill on the field of forensics, however, I was triumphant once I had no opponent, and accordingly I propose a Walter Mitty-like digest of what I might have said to the lady novelist if I had ever found an opening. First I might notice an unpleasant feeling I had while her deluge continued. I kept thinking of automatic gear shifts. I recalled my own feelings when the things were invented. I had learned to shift gears on a Model-T Ford, added a Druxel axle, transferred to the old Dodge shift, then the standard and Paige shifts, and finally learned to double-clutch a truck. I resented the whole notion of automatic gear shifts. I told myself that I could shift better than any danged gadget, and that I wanted my car to shift when I wanted it to shift, not when it wanted to shift. But all this time I knew I was giving sanctuary to a sneaking notion that having learned the hard way I did not want my precious skill to become obsolete while other people learned an easier way. Now I may do the lady injustice, but I thought I detected a similar note in her argument, that she had learned what she knew with great difficulty and she did not want anybody else learning more easily.

If, however, I am uncertain where her reasoning left off and her rationalizing began, I am quite sure of the essential differences between us: she had little notion of how creative writing is taught. We did not agree as to why one might teach creative writing, and her notions of what constitutes teaching were quite different from mine. In the first place, she was convinced that teachers of creative writing spend their time disseminating matter which has little to do with anything but imaginative journalism, and insofar as this is true she had a point. She very rightly said that writing is more than learning a few tricks of the trade, although I would insist that even teaching of this sort has some use. For instance, readers become nervous when the point of view shifts, and young writers incline too much to shift their points of view; they do well to avoid shifting more than they must, and there are devices which an old pro can show them and which may save agony, blundering, and rejection slips. Quite possibly, counselling of this nature is in the end a specious sort of help. Some writers will perhaps learn more if they are never given any good advice, if they sharpen their brains learning everything the hard way, and know what they know the better for having the conviction that they invented everything themselves and that all knowledge began with them.

Personally, I doubt that this is true of many writers. Certainly it is not the principle on which publishers and editors work, and I suspect that for most writers, beginning or otherwise, something always remains to be learned about structure and method, and that no serious writer is ever the worse for a bit of timely advice. But at least this much can be conceded, that part of the profession of pedagogy is knowing—if one ever can know—what to do and what not to do and thereby to force the student to do it for himself, and that pedagogic doubt must remain as to how much good a teacher does instructing students in methodology, provided they are concerned with something more than tailoring hack stories to predetermined markets.

Now to our second difference, as to why creative writing may be taught. I conceded at once that it should not be the purpose of the teacher at any level to make two creative writers grow where only one grew before. I conceded also that there are too many creative writers already, and that some of them might well find other ways to earn a living—although I noticed that my assailant, while asserting that the number of creative writers should be reduced, was not assuming that she was one of the writers who should be liquidated. I would even have conceded that most young people to whom instruction is offered are not creative writers and that they show no considerable promise of becoming Shakespeares or even Hemingways. But I still believe in encouraging them. I would suggest by way of analogy that most of the young people to whom instruction in music is offered will not become Beethovens or Paderewskis, and that whatever the ambitions of these young people may be, many of their parents know quite well when they pay for the music lessons that they are paying for music appreciation, not mainly for the perfection of creative musical genius.

Similarly, I believe that one of the great needs of our day is a larger body of more discriminating readers who will and can understand what a good writer is saying. I know of no better way to cultivate such a body of readers than to encourage intelligent young people to try a bit of serious writing themselves, however gruesome the written results may be. Once a young person has endeavored to search within himself for whatever may be most worth saying and to give something like memorable expression to this vague stuff that men and dreams are made of, he will never be quite so intellectually naive again in artistic matters. He will not thereafter so readily believe, as many Americans now believe, that people write because, once a book is published, the author waxes fabulously wealthy, and that creativity is a pleasant by-product of drugs and whisky, so that a writer need only become drunk enough and stay drunk long enough to produce another *War and Peace*.

And now for my main point of disagreement. When my assailant said that nobody can teach anything worth learning about creative writing I suspect that she was using the word *teach* differently than most of us use it. She was assuming that teaching is about what was implied in that classic definition of the lecture method, that method by which the contents of the teacher's notes get into the student's notes without passing through the brains of either. I grant that if we could here call up the ghost of Homer and he were to deliver us a brilliant and cogent lecture on the writing of epics, we should not thereafter set about out-Homering Homer, that we should thereafter write not much better and not much worse and not even much differently. Little creativity can be taught by lecturing, whether the medium be poetry, music, or unsculptured stone, but art can be encouraged, I believe by precept and by sympathetic atmosphere. Being a creative person, however unsuccessful in the world's eyes, and providing an atmosphere congenial to creativity is what I mean by teaching creative writing, or mainly what I mean. There may be artists whose milk of human kindness is turned to green bile by the sight of another artist, and for whom sympathetic understanding is the most diabolical of the devil's works, but I am convinced that they are few, and that they are especially few among young creative people who are still groping. Most artists and would-be artists dreadfully need the sense that somebody knows what they are trying to do, and they need even more dreadfully the fellow association of people who know why they must grope. If a teacher of creative writing can do no more than to bring such young people together he has earned his pay check; if he can himself stand for intelligence and integrity in art he has done even more; and if, as is I believe rather frequent, he can see more clearly than anybody else whom the student encounters what the student meant to do but did not, and what the student did that was most worth treasuring and improving upon, then he is an extremely useful teacher indeed. The established writer can find an artistic community in his reviews, his fan mail, his royalty statements, and his literary friendships, but the beginner, if he finds sympathetic understanding at all, is likely to find it among his baffled contemporaries and with some older person who starts as his teacher and becomes his fellow student of writing.

Offerings in creative writing may be as formally organized as the writing school at Iowa, or they may be as informal as that poetry group which used to meet during the pre-writing school days at Iowa in the office of the late Edwin Ford Piper. Nobody got any credit and nobody was expected to attend, but it was known that "Pipe" would always be in his office Saturday at ten. If you went there with a poem in your pocket it would be read and other would-be poets would talk about it, and Pipe himself, with his very great understanding and kindness would say something helpful and not too harsh. Looking back on my own attendance at those sessions I am convinced that I learned more from Pipe being understanding at ten on Saturday than I had from most of my instructors lecturing all week. Of course a teacher of creative writing never knows when he is teaching anything worth teaching, and if he is. The promising youngster who becomes an established novelist might have become a better novelist without advice, and he might have become a better psychiatrist than he is a novelist if he had not been given the help that led to the acceptance of his first book. But that is the bane of all teaching. We do not know whether we are training senators or super-gangsters, whether in promoting the making of engineers we are salvaging or sinking mankind. A teacher can only hope he is a benefactor. But so far as my personal observation is valid, I find that I can do more of what I believe in and less of what I am doubtful about when I attempt to teach creative writing than in most of the other subjects I have tried or have seen others try.

⟶❦ 16. ❧⟵

The Case for Casebooks: One Way to Handle the Research Paper

As is indicated in lecture 11, "Language History," I believe that the use of casebooks to promote objective writing in the secondary schools has been long and inexplicably delayed. Such collections of source materials have triggered a minor revolution in the teaching of composition in college, but as yet they are almost unknown in secondary schools, and the attempts—including my own —to introduce them to secondary-school teachers have been dismal failures. Some day casebooks will engender an even greater reform in high schools than they have promoted in colleges, but at this writing that day is not yet.

Ginn High School English Notes, no. 8 (1966), pp. 1–3, 7.

How should one teach objective, factual writing in the secondary schools? This question disturbs many teachers, many of the best teachers. It came sharply to my attention at the convention of the Idaho Council of the Teachers of English last November. Hoping to stimulate discussion I had distributed what I called "The Ten Commandments of English Composition." One was as follows:

> Thou shalt teach thy students not to steal; students should learn to respect intellectual property and intellectual integrity, and they should learn the means of embodying this respect in their thinking and writing; they should learn to deal objectively with the writing of others, and they should master the techniques by which a writer makes known his awareness of the uncertainty and mystery of a world in which fact is always shot through with error, in which truth is always qualified.

This was probably not the most important of my commandments, but apparently it came closer to the teachers' concerns than did most of the others. At least it was the only one of the ten that stimulated every group to whom I talked. I remember particularly the exchange that resulted from one teacher's question.

"Why do the colleges not want us to teach the research paper?" she asked.

The question may have been loaded a bit. The teacher possibly implied, "Why do you college teachers not appreciate the good work we are doing in the high schools?" but I think not, at least not much. The teacher had the earmarks of a good one—alert, literate, and probably devoted. Furthermore, I could sense that the group was involved; they wanted to see if I could say anything that would make sense.

Accordingly, I tried. First, I pointed out that "the colleges"

are not one thing with one set of beliefs about anything, and that
I could not speak for all of them. I added that many college teachers believe that the so-called research paper should not be taught to
beginners anywhere, in high school or in college, but I had to admit
that these adverse critics object especially to the teaching of the
research paper in secondary schools. For this objection, I suggested
two main reasons.

First, the freshmen who arrive in college do not know how to
write objectively, or at least most of them do not, in spite of the
fact that some of them have written what are called research papers.
On the whole, these students have been asked to write down what
they think, but they have not been shown how to record what someone else thinks. They are likely not even to understand that objective writing can be a goal, to say nothing of ever having learned to
do such writing. Many college teachers would suggest that the
proper role of the composition course in high school—or one of the
roles—is to teach objective writing on a relatively simple level.
Once the student has learned straightforward, objective writing, he
can go on to the more elaborate techniques involved in the reporting of research, but most college teachers feel that the teaching of
research procedures is relatively meaningless until the student has
learned to do objective writing.

Second, many college teachers believe that teaching the research paper in any superficial way does positive harm, and that,
with some gratifying exceptions, the research paper is generally
taught superficially. Here I recounted an experience of my own. I
had been teaching in a summer session in a nearby city, where our
paperboy learned that I was a professor of English. He asked me if
I would help him with his research paper: could I recommend a
book on the Russian novel? I asked him what Russian novel; surely
he was not writing on all of them. Oh, yes; and what would be a
book he could get some quotes out of? I asked him what Russian
novels he had read. He seemed to consider this question not worth
answering, but when I pressed the point he said he did not have
time to read any now—maybe later. He was too busy writing the
paper. I had to tell him that if he were my student I should insist
that he restrict himself to one novel, or at the worst to one novelist,
and that he start by reading the novels.

Obviously by now I had lost caste, but he was a patient and polite young man. He explained that I did not know how these things are done. Usually, the way you wrote a research paper was to copy things out of several encyclopedias. That was what the other pupils were doing, but he wanted to get an "A" so he was going to read a book along with the encyclopedia articles, or part of a book anyhow, maybe parts of two or three if they were not very long parts.

I asked him about the course he was taking. It seems it was a special honors course, given in the summer to selected students. He was lucky to be in it. Eventually, we parted with me still suggesting that he ought to read any novels he discussed, and that it might be a good idea to talk with his teacher about the books he should consult, but that if he was only going to use books about novels, he could find some through the card catalogue in the city library. I did not see him again until just before we were leaving, when he stopped to thank me for my help and to tell me that he had received his "A" in the course, and the teacher had written "Very good" on the paper. I tried to act pleased, although I am not sure I was very convincing.

Unfortunately, I could not ignore this incident as evidence of the follies of American school systems. The local schools have an excellent reputation, and I have reason to believe that this fame is justified. Furthermore, the case cannot be dismissed as involving a substandard course taught by a beginner who doubled as basketball coach; the course was a show piece, an example of enrichment. Obviously, the teacher must have enjoyed the respect of the administration, and I had to observe that he had the opportunity to teach the research paper if he had wanted to, for my little friend could have been taught elementary research, provided that was desirable. He was bright and zealous to learn, but far from being taught how to do research he was being taught how not to do it. In fact, he was being taught how not to practice elementary intellectual honesty. I have been troubled about him ever since.

Having told my little story to the Idaho teachers, I was glad to concede that some secondary instructors are teaching the research paper well, but I had to add that the annual crop of college freshmen confirms the fear in many professors that good pupils in good schools are being corrupted, and that in poor schools with lesser pupils the state of learning must be even worse. One reason, of course, is that many high-school teachers have themselves done no serious research, and how can they be expected to teach what they have not experienced? Our teacher-training programs being what they are, we must expect that many teachers will have no real understanding of what research is or how it should be taught. Accordingly, to get back to the original question, I admitted that many college teachers would say that teaching the research paper in secondary schools is a dubious practice at best, and under present conditions, generally inadvisable.

At this point my interlocutor demonstrated that she was asking serious questions. What could the high school teacher do?

I replied that in college we have lately received good help from what are called casebooks for controlled research materials. These volumes stem from two that were started some ten years ago, almost simultaneously by two publishing houses. The idea was that the editor would choose a moderately restricted but interesting subject, the London fire, for example, the witch-burning in New England, or symbolism in *The Red Badge of Courage*. He would then reprint in an inexpensive, paperbound volume, selections from sources concerning the topic, and would supply apparatus for studying these materials and using them for papers. The volume called *London in Plague and Fire* reprints parts of the diaries of Samuel Pepys and John Evelyn, the writings of contemporary physicians, the anathemas from clergymen who were convinced that the plague was the scourge of God, personal letters, newspaper accounts, official death lists, and the like.

Presumably these collections have several virtues. They reduce the confusion in the library, when hundreds or thousands of freshmen, who have never labored in a card catalogue until now, descend upon the librarians wanting to know if they have a book on witches, or our foreign policy, or the evils of communism in China. The casebooks would also assure that all students would have a usable body of source materials, however inadequate the library. The books could be used to obviate plagiarism; since the teacher would know what sources the student had used, he could tell at once whether sources had been used properly and could respond accordingly. And best of all, since the whole class would be working on a common body of material, the teacher could devise writing projects which would teach the techniques of objective writing one by one. Thus the student would be learning the fundamentals of the most important sort of modern writing, objective writing, and at the same time he would be weaned from plagiarism by learning how to handle quoted material properly.

The casebooks were an immediate success. College teachers demanded them faster than the presses could produce them, and most publishers of college English texts developed series of controlled research materials. These ballooned so rapidly that by now college teachers can select from nearly two hundred titles, and the end is not near. Meanwhile, not all teachers have been converted to the new books. Some instructors point out that a paper written from controlled research materials does not teach use of the library, and some of these teachers feel that skill in library reference work is the chief end of the research paper, or at least one of its most important by-products. Other teachers have mitigated this shortcoming by having their students use the casebooks to learn the techniques of objective writing, and thereafter have made assignments which require library work. Some teachers have found that the casebooks can become boring, and with reason. By the time a teacher has read a few hundred papers on one subject, even the London fire or Pickett's charge could become boring, but at the college level this difficulty has been overcome. The teacher can use different casebooks for different sections, and can change them every semester if he wishes. Many teachers have found that two casebooks a semester work out well: a relatively easy, objctive book to teach simple skills and a more difficult set of materials dealing with ideas, critical concepts, and the like.

Clearly, everything that has endeared these casebooks to many college teachers should make them even more welcome to high-school teachers, who, on the whole, have had less training in research, poorer libraries to work with, fewer selected students, and heavier teaching loads. Until now, casebooks for writing have not been much used in secondary schools, for which there may be several reasons. Most high school teachers, I find, have never heard of them, partly because most high school salesmen have no such books to sell. Many high school teachers would not have known what to do with them if they had had them; they would have assumed that the book on the London plague should be used in social studies class. Indeed it could be, but it would achieve its main purpose only if it was used as a writing book, not as a bit of added information in a history unit. True, after a pupil has worked over the documents and has tried to generalize from them, he is likely to develop understanding of seventeenth-century history, or social organization, and even of human psychology that had formerly been beyond him, but he will do so because he has used the materials to write from, not because he has been tempted with "extra credit" for additional reading.

[In the original essay, I predicted that within five years the secondary schools would have at their disposal floods of casebooks for objective writing. Those five years have now elapsed, and I must concede that during a distended history of disgruntled prophesying, I have seldom done worse. But someday time will justify me; casebooks are so appropriate to high school learning that sometime, somewhere, they must be discovered.]

–◀ 17. ▶–

Reading and Writing

In February, 1968, I was scheduled to speak before the Toronto Council of the International Reading Association, at the invitation of the conference and of the Language Study Center for the Toronto school system. Through some confusion I thought they had suggested the title that appears above; I wrote the paper for them and read it to them, and not until later did I discover that this was not what they had expected at all. For me it was a fortunate confusion; the Toronto people were gracious about it, and they got me to thinking along lines that I would probably not have had the wit to suggest myself. The piece has not previously been offered for publication.

A legendary bird, supposedly native to India, is said to have but one wing, and accordingly can fly only in pairs. The existence of this startling ornithological specimen was reported to me by a former fiancée, shortly after our engagement. I was charmed by the idea, although I can now admit, what I did not at the time care to mention to my intended, that I puzzled a bit over the problems of aviarial dynamics with which these inconveniently constructed fowls must have found themselves involved. Supporting weight by beating the air occasions a great variety of thrusts and surges, and I could not help wondering what sort of lock or jointure would be needed to turn the lopsided thrashings of these creatures into smooth flight. So long as one considers the birds analogically and not anatomically, I assume that the link between them is provided by matrimony, and at the time I was enough absorbed in the uses of marriage to leave it at that. I fear, however, that I am too mundane or too much the son of the twentieth century to become permanently divorced from the realities of a sensuous world. For this or some other reason, I was never entirely happy about those birds.

More recently, speculating upon the relationships between reading and writing, I have recalled these legendary mates and their peculiar problems of interdependence. I am not suggesting that such ornithological marvels provide a perfect comparison for communication skills. If reading and writing are interreliant they are not that interreliant. Some people who can read cannot, in effect, write, and in theory a scribe could perform the mechanical operation of writing without being able to read the result, but practically speaking, the two go together. Almost never does an individual practice one extensively without being able to employ the other, and I am convinced that the two are closely linked in the learning process, more closely linked than most of us realize.

If this be true, then the linkage between them is a matter of some concern, particularly to those of us who profess the language arts.

Pretty obviously, the link is complex, at least as complex as the jointure that would have been required by those legendary flying mates, for complicated as flight may be, communication is even more complex and the working of its components more subtle. Some portions of this linkage are unmistakable. One is language; both readers and writers must use language as their tool, written as well as oral language, however they learn to command it. Another is the power to conceptualize, however this power is developed. A third is command of the grammatical and rhetorical patterns of the language as these are employed in sentence structures, in the smaller patterns within the sentence, and probably in the larger patterns, whether we think of these in terms of paragraphs and what some writers call "stadia," or whether we treat them as aspects of what the tagmemists call wave and field. I speak of this linguistic trinity as though each were distinct, separate, and self-contained. They are not, of course. The last two may be thought of as aspects or parts of the first, but as teachers we may wish to consider them as though they are entities, at least these three: language and language learning, the power to conceptualize, and the patterns of composition.

First to language. Here we should note that language, in whatever form it is used and for whatever purpose, is essentially an activity of the mind. As it appears, of course, it uses other portions of our anatomies, and these appearances are so much the more obvious that we tend to think of them as the major media of speech. We read with our eyes, hear with our ears, write with our fingers and arms, and speak with the various portions of our oral-respiratory tract. Most of us are not much aware of the workings of these organs and our other facilities; I confess I do not know what would happen to my hearing if the anvils in my middle ears should cease to function. Most speakers know nothing of the workings of chest and abdominal muscles that control the flow of breath, cannot consciously voice or unvoice a sound, and are unaware that years of self-imposed though unconscious training went into their ability to control that difficult muscle, the tongue. Furthermore, as teachers we can observe that the control of these speech facilities seems to be not much our professional business; as Words-worth has observed, the ear cannot help but hear, and even control of the tongue is mastered by small children without much of our instruction.

This raises the question of what is our business in teaching the use of the native language. Superficially, the answer is easy. We need not teach what the students will learn best without our help; on the other hand, we need to teach what the students need or will need, but are not likely to learn, or learn economically, or learn at the right time by themselves. Here we should notice a peculiarity of language learning as contrasted with almost all other sorts of intellectual learning, that it is unconscious and not mainly deliberate. Almost all the chemistry that a child learns he learns deliberately, and the process is mainly directed by the teacher. Most language is learned unconsciously and the teacher has nothing to do with it; there is so much of it to be learned that most of it can, in effect, be learned in no other way. That is, language is mainly learned by unconscious imitation. Our job, teaching some language by instruction and by more or less consciously directed activity, is a small part of the whole process of language learning, but so important is language as an intellectual and social power, so difficult is the command of language, and so crucial for language proficiency are some portions of the formal study and practice of language, that our responsibility, as we all know, is profound.

[The original here included a discussion of grammar that needs teaching, as against grammar that does not, and of learning language as wholes; see lecture 12, "Seen but not Heard," above.]

Now to conceptualization. Here we are dealing with one of the fundamentals of language, vocabulary. All languages have some sort of linguistic units which are involved, among other things, with meaning, and this formulation of meaning is fundamental in language learning and language use. The study of formulation of meaning is what is coming to be called psycholinguistics. With much of it we need not concern ourselves; it falls within the area of unconscious learning, which is the child's business, not ours. All children learn the equivalent of *Mommy* and *Daddy*; at an early age the child conceives these objects as large and of the sort he sees around him, and he distinguishes them by differences in voice, clothes, hair, and the like. Obviously he has no notion of distinguishing them on the basis of sex, procreation of the species, marital relationship, or any of the other major concepts that an adult might use in making distinctions. The child conceptualizes unconsciously on his childish level, but he will continue to revise that inadequate concept without much help from anyone. By the time of puberty his concept of the creature he called *Mommy* will have changed markedly, and these concepts will continue to change, without much need of formal teaching and without much impact from formal teaching. That is, conceptualizing is a lifelong process, and for some words and phrases it follows naturally from the ways of a mind with life and language.

This process does not, however, work for most words. As the child grows to maturity, if he is to move in a cultured society or assume business or professional responsibilities of any complexity, he is deluged with words which he must learn to command, but which he has not learned and cannot learn naturally in his home or on the playground. They are not used there, or if they are known and used at all they are not employed sufficiently so that he can form and refine his concepts as he does those for *Mommy* and *dinner*.

Formerly, this limitation was less operative. Few children were highly educated, and these were, on the whole, the offspring of educated parents. They lived in homes where sophisticated conversation was the rule, and this conversation was carried on at least partly in their presence; the dinner table, for example, was in those vanished days an institution not associated with a televised Mickey Mouse. All this is changed. We now endeavor to educate a large proportion of our population, and these young people mainly live in households where the adults do not command adult vocabularies, or if they do, they do not practice them much in the presence of their children.

Pretty obviously, here is one of the areas in which the modern teacher of the native language must ask himself what his responsibility is and how he can best rise to this need. He must encourage natural learning of vocabulary, even though by unnatural means, and he must consider what he should do to teach conceptualization formally and consciously. Determining the best procedures here is more your business than mine, but I can suggest that at least one way to teach vocabulary naturally is to encourage wide reading, reading of material not very familiar to the student, lots of such reading. If the student does not frequently encounter words like *instigate, redaction,* and *simplistic* in conversations related to the basketball court or the soccer field, he can be induced to read written material in which these and similar words occur in context and occur frequently enough so that he can learn them, as he learns best, by acquiring wholes. We can also teach him such words deliberately. Here, of course, the tried and true method of studying prefixes and suffixes can help, but I surmise that even more useful are several less recognized disciplines like etymology and semantics.

Now to my third area, that of the more complex patterns of composition. These, on the whole, the modern child does not learn naturally, at least not enough and not well enough. The basic patterns he learns. He learns the sequence of determiner, modifier, noun, and he is never in error or at a loss here. He never says "blue the jeans" or "motor old an," nor does he have to hesitate in his choice of word order. He distinguishes the interrogative, declarative, and imperative sentence patterns flawlessly and without conscious thought, but he does not learn to write in paragraphs. He does not learn the complex patterns of subordination because these are not known to the children with whom he associates, or if they are sporadically known they are not used on playing fields or in youthful small talk. These patterns of adult communication, however, are essential to modern serious reading and writing. The growing student finds that he needs them; he needs them in all their multifarious complexity, and he needs to acquire them much more rapidly than he is likely to, using only his unaided powers of imitation. Here, once more, the teacher of the native language should enter, and he should arrive knowing what his job is and how he should fill it. And here, also, one is struck by the same fundamental fact, that when the teacher searches for methods he is likely to find that part of his help comes from the interreliance of language use, of the learning by wholes through both reading and writing.

That is, the roots of writing and reading are both so firmly intertwined in the same earth, in language and the fundamental processes of language, that we should expect them to be somewhat interdependent, or at least that they would respond to the same stimuli. This we would assume, theoretically, even though we knew nothing practically about the way reading and writing work and how they are learned. My own experience, and I am sure the experience of many others, suggests that reading and writing are in fact interreliant as they are learned and used by the individual.

For example, I have long been forced to recognize that most incoming Freshmen, at least in the institutions in which I have taught, can neither read nor write well, partly because they do not understand what a paragraph is, how it is made, nor how it should be used. I find I can start the teaching of the paragraph most expeditiously by encouraging close reading. I make the student analyze written paragraph after written paragraph until he can recognize the characteristics of the basic expository paragraph and can describe the common variations upon such a formula. Next I try to induce him to write paragraphs, partly by using good written paragraphs as models. I then find that once he has learned to construct an orderly paragraph himself he can understand the paragraphs written by others and do so with a precision and expedition which would previously have been foreign to him. That is, I find I can teach reading and writing together better than I can teach either alone.

Fortunately I need not rely solely on my personal impressions. Some years ago I was involved in an experiment at the University of Oregon which produced tolerably measurable evidence. [This experiment is described in lecture 20, "A Do-It-Yourself Program," below.]

The results were modestly positive. The tests showed that the students taught by this method did indeed improve their written composition somewhat more than did control groups who were taught by two other methods. This did not surprise those of us who believed in the new method, but what did surprise all of us was a side effect. The students who had improved in writing by this method improved even more in reading. As I say, this fact surprised me at the time but it puzzles me no longer. I believe I see now that in order to criticize the compositions of their contemporaries, students had been induced to read written work more carefully than they had ever read before, with the resultant improvement in their reading generally.

To put all this briefly, as every teacher knows, we learn by doing. We learn to write by writing, and we learn to read by reading. But at the same time, we learn each by doing the other. That this is so need not surprise us. After all, both use the same medium, language, and both spring from similar mental processes. Both must make use of the same human devices, of learning by imitation, for example, and of learning by linguistic wholes. Of course we, as teachers, have to know something of the nature of language and of language learning; we need to distinguish what is our business from what is not our business. With such aids we can greatly enhance our teaching, and notably through making use of the interreliance of the various uses of language, including writing and reading.

--◄ 18. ►--

Three Whimsies
Concerning Literature for the Many

This paper, not previously published, was written in the early 1940s for an institute at what is now Utah State University. Rereading it now I am surprised to find how much it has dated in superficialities, but how little in essentials. I was younger and brasher in those days, and I notice that the style contrasts with that in more recent pieces, but I also notice that I still believe most of what I said a quarter of a century ago, and I seem to have said it with rather more vigor then than I now command. Accordingly, I have not tried to modernize the lecture much, although the school system has improved sufficiently so that where I have written *college freshman* one can now read *high school senior*.

—◦◦❦ A former teacher of mine once made the fruitful suggestion that anybody who writes and publishes a book should be beheaded. Whether he spoke surveying his own list of published works, I know not, but I fear he may have wished some kind legislator had saved him from the fate worse than death—that of becoming a prostituted author. He could, however, offer reasons to support his plan. No more, he might say, would Edgar Rice Burroughs trouble the young mind, struggling to distinguish between Tarzan and Tarzan's fellow apes. No more would noble fir trees become ignoble comic strips. No more would Hendrik Willem Van Loon [whom few readers will now recall] produce semiannual masterpieces. We should have done with mediocre books. For most men weigh the worth of their heads, however lightly they ponder their printed words. If a man knew he would lose his head for it, never would he publish a book until he was quite sure he had something to say, quite sure he would never again have anything so important to say, quite sure he had learned all he ever would learn about his subject. Furthermore, most of our books would then come from those great and noble souls who would willingly lay down their heads for humanity. Our libraries might be smaller, but they would be more carefully selected at the source.

Now, if this be due treatment for the author of a book, quite otherwise is it with a teacher addressing an audience—or at least so I am convinced while reading a lecture myself. Not even my blood-thirsty, one-time professor suggested that a man be decapitated for reading a paper—provided it was not a dull paper—and I have concluded that, while a book should contain as much truth as possible, a paper should avoid anything so sober as the truth, and should be a tissue of improbable plausibilities. Such a paper has advantages; it stirs the listeners to wrath and retort while it ventilates the soul of the speaker, who may amuse himself without a sense of responsibility. Consider, for instance, the sad case of Pontius Pilate. He confused the essential character of a book and a paper. He asked, we are told, "What is truth?" and was so indiscreet as to raise the question in open meeting. Now, had he written a book on the subject, the book would have been burned with the great library at Alexandria, and he would have remained in the relative peace of a minor Roman official notable for an occasional convenient crucifixion. But since he confused the proper functions of a book and a paper, his name has become a byword for jesting at truth. Lest my name, also, become a byword, I shall avoid truth and confine myself to the whimsies of what I hope you may charitably assume is a mind at play.

The first whimsy, then, is that literature is tremendously and vitally important. At this point I should remind myself that literature is the most understandable of the arts, because it employs the artistic medium most understandable to us, the words which we as a race have made. It is possible to discover, within reasonable limits, what Shakespeare, for instance, said in a given line and approximately what he meant when he said it. Not so with the other arts. Beethoven may have known what he wanted to say in a sonata; Nijinsky may have known how he felt in a certain dance; individuals of us may at times have a conviction that we know what these men were trying to say. But tone, rhythm, and movement have no exact, definable values, and it is very unlikely that any two of us will be able to agree as to what Beethoven and Nijinsky actually did succeed in saying.

Nor is art without importance. Not unless mankind is without importance, unless civilization is without importance, unless culture is without importance. For with no will to create, man as we think of him would scarcely be. Without the desire to make something, just for the fun of making it, we should be hopping about on two or more legs, squawking and squeaking like the rest of creation. And art is perhaps the highest form in which this creative spirit expresses itself. If we want to know why we act like human animals instead of acting like other animals, if we want to sense the long change of the animal into the cultured human, then we must study art, for art is our most studiable form of the driving force that made us civilized. Art shows us why we are what we are. Literature, as I have tried to suggest, is the most understandable of the arts, and thus the most understandable example in a highly developed form of the vital urge that has made us, as a civilization and as civilized individuals.

Literature offers the integrated approach to life. I have sometimes wondered at modernists in education, who have stuffed curricula with trivia from Hairdressing to How to Coach Football, while throwing out literature, and then have complained because education has no integration. I have wondered at these educators, too, when they marvel that the schools of the past five hundred years have done so well, although the courses of study were so bad. The answer, I am convinced, is that the old curricula were not bad, partly because they were saturated with literature, and literature offers the integrated approach to most of what man needs to know. Now I grant you that certain essentially analytic subjects are necessary, especially in technical training. The method of science is analysis, or at best, synthesis preceded by analysis. The method of professional training is analysis, followed by intensive work which uses synthesis as only one of its approaches. Scientific study and professional training we must have, and under their influence our world is becoming more and more specialized, more and more departmentalized, more and more cut up into seemingly irrelated bits. And this will go on. Thus, more and more, man needs a method of studying which offers a synthesis, an approach which integrates his diverse studies and his life, too. For this study, literature offers the most useful and the most usable material.

Permit me to be specific. I happen to be teaching a section of modern literature in which one of the required books is Franz Werfel's *Forty Days of Musa Dagh*. When the youngsters have finished it, they have done much more than spend a few pleasant hours. They have made a sizable start on at least the following courses: Geology 123, Geography of the Near East; Ethnology 169, Acculturation Problems; Political Science 2, Organization and Functioning of States; Psychology 3, Problems in Modern Psychology; Sociology 78, Races and Racial Mixing; Sociology 161, Marriage. Best of all, they have learned to think of all these things directly, basing what they learn on their own experience, not seeing what they see darkly, through the fog of course-numbers. They will never again be able to think of the east coast of the Mediterranean as a pink blob on the map, inhabited by Mohammedans with long, curved swords and the morals of a male cockroach. They will be better prepared to take their place in a world that is more and more an international world. The words "Pan-Arab Problem" will no longer be just words; they will stand for a problem that is real and human. And when the time comes, as I hope it may after this war, to do something about the Pan-Arab problem, they will be a bit better prepared to give the question the kind of consideration it must have, if the democracies are to make a workable world this time, in a democratic way. [The problem has been exacerbated although not fundamentally much altered by the growth of the state of Israel.]

So much for my first whimsy, that literature and the study of literature are dreadfully important in our day. My second whimsy may seem even less plausible, that most lower division students do not know what literature is. At times I fear there are teachers who do not know what literature is, and in my lugubrious moments I wonder if I can be one of those teachers. But if I do not know what literature is, I feel fairly sure I know some things it is not, yet every year I see a large percentage of my students accepting as literature something that it certainly is not. These students come from good homes; they are approved by our secondary schools and have done college work; individually they seem to be good students. Yet they do not know literature when they see it, and all too frequently, if they like the right things they like them for the wrong reasons. They praise verse because the rhythm can be made to thump, because the lines rhyme, and because the whole embodies moral notions congenial to the local mores. They prefer that it deal with Mother, skylarks, love, or houses by the side of the road. Now whatever poetry may be, that, I know, is not the definition of poetry. Similarly, these students praise a novel if it offers what they are looking for: chaste kisses and wedding bells toward the end of the book; descriptions of nature, so long as nature has no bad smells; improbable adventures, and plenty of noble souls. If there are bad people in the book, they must be bad only in certain ways; they may commit murder, for instance; they may lie, and cheat, and steal, so long as they remember the wedding vow to keep it holy. Now, whatever a novel may be, these, again, are not the requisites of a good novel.

[I have let the previous paragraph stand, partly to highlight a change, partly to suggest that the more it changes the more it is the same. The students described here still exist, but they are relatively fewer, and have been replaced by the offspring of my former students, many of whom demand that a novel be a flood of violence, copulation, and perversion. If they are more sophisticated than their parents, they are not much more sophisticated; Mickey Spillane is probably not closer to being a novelist than was Harold Bell Wright. Some change there has been; the whole country has matured, the school systems have been improved, the paperback books have in part supplanted popular periodicals, but perhaps the most interesting aspect of the previous paragraph is this, that although students have vastly enhanced their superficial qualities during the last quarter of a century their grasp of literary art and its significance has altered much less.]

At this point I wish to record a curious fact. Although many a student seems to me fundamentally wrong on a basic question, he is a rare young man who doubts that he knows what literature is. He may believe that literature is hard for him—he says he can't "get literature," as a sinner might say he could not "get religion"— but he blandly asumes that he knows what he ought to get. In fact a student sometimes reveals as much, usually after I have carelessly given him an *F*. "I guess I can't get literature," he will say. On these occasions I often fear that the student is being polite and considerate of my feelings. What he really means to say is something like this: "I guess I can't get what you want me to get; I used to be able to get literature, but the way you teach it, I don't seem to get it." Accordingly, I try to find out what he means by literature. The obvious answer is that he expects to receive at least an average grade in a course labeled literature; but pressed a little further, the student may reveal that for him literature is knowing who died in 1616 and that Milton got his daughters out of bed at night to dictate *Paradise Lost* to them. The implication is, I take it, that I have not played the game according to the rules, for the conscientious student has told me about Milton's daughters losing their beauty sleeps, yet I have not been impressed. If at this point

I try to explain that the conscientious student has not understood the content of the course; that the course is literature, that literature is more than knowing how, for Milton's daughters, *Paradise Lost* was just the rather dull hobby of a bothersome old man who happened to be their father. If I am so indiscreet as to try to say something of this sort, I usually encounter a wall of tradition. Years of courses labeled literature have convinced the student that he knows what literature is, and I have some trouble convincing him that what he means by literature is not what Homer, or Marlowe, or Shelley, or Tolstoy, or James Joyce, or T. S. Eliot meant by literature. Not that I object to dates and the learning of dates. On the contrary. But I do object to confusing the trappings of literature, the circumstances of literature, the tools one uses in studying literature, with the literature itself.

Usually I do not blame the youngster. He may be one of those happy creatures whom the Lord in his wisdom has created without the irritation of a brain. More frequently I feel that the student just never has been told, at least not in a way he could understand and feel. Nobody has told him that literature is the distilled essence of mankind, that when men's hearts are wrung, poems come out of them. Nobody ever told him that men ache, and long, and cry after beauty, or peace, or understanding, and that when they do, something of what they feel may take form and become a lyric or a novel. Nobody ever showed him what it means to feel a book big within you, to know that there is that gestating which could be for thousands unborn a truth that they had not known; nobody revealed what it does to people to know that such an artistic birth may be, to know that it must be loved, and cherished, and fought for, and fought over, if it is to come to man's estate, that one can love a novel as he loves a baby. Or if the student has been told, he has never understood that literature is life, and that it is torn raw and bleeding from the best of men. Probably, he has not even been told that "Poetry is the record of the best and happiest moments of the happiest and best minds," that literature results when noble spirits "see life steadily and see it whole." He has learned that Coleridge wrote poetry because he ate opium, and that literature is knowing who wrote *Huckleberry Finn*.

[I have let the paragraph above stand, also; it is not so valid as it was, but it remains after a quarter century, more valid than I could wish.]

So much for my second whimsy, that many students in junior college have not been told, in a way understandable to them, what literature is. Now, my third improbability is that literature can be taught to freshmen and sophomores, and that with these students we can do something genuinely important for American culture. I do not know whether or not literature can be taught generally in the high schools in the near future. [Both teachers and students are improving; see the headnote.] I do know that certain high school teachers can teach literature to certain high school students, but I know also that in most of the high schools sending their product to my own institution, literature is not being apprehended. I do not blame the high schools. They labor under difficulties. I fear, however, that most high schools have not taught literature, as I have tried to describe it, to most of their students. Thus, while I have a settled conviction that literature can be taught in the high school, and even in the grade schools, (at least to a substantial percentage of the students), I harbor a stubborn doubt that literature will be taught soon in many high schools to most of the students, however desirable this teaching may be, however many courses are labeled literature, however excellent the work done by certain teachers with certain students.

Happily, junior colleges [and the newly developed community colleges] are more favored. Students are a little older; they are beginning to have the experiences that are the stuff of adult life, and thus the stuff of the bulk of literature. They are better able to feel and to understand. They are more highly selected, for many of the unteachables have fallen by the way. In short, the junior college student ought to be capable of understanding that literature is refined human experience, made memorable and significant through the alchemy of a skilled literary artist. Junior college teachers ought to be able to teach that literature is life made more understandable, that it is experience which helps one to mature and grow emotionally, that it is knowledge made human and humanity made significant. I might add that my own acquaintance with junior college teaching leads me to believe that most students can be taught so much, and that my acquaintance with graduate schools convinces me that teachers to do this job are available, at least in moderate quantities. I regret to add that they are not always the teachers who most easily find good jobs.

However that may be, in the junior college we have the best chance to teach literature to most of the important people of the next generation. The average young person does not receive a degree these days; even the average intelligent young person does not receive a degree. But most of those who will amount to something eventually do start some collegiate work. For most of these people, on the other hand, junior college courses offer the last opportunity they will ever have to receive formal help in the arts or the humanities. In my own institution, for instance, many fewer than half of those who register for junior college work take upper division work there or anywhere else. Of those who do take more advanced work, the majority are engaged in vocational, technical, or professional training that provides for very little acquaintance with the arts and the humanities. Probably four out of five, perhaps five out of six of the students that enter our doors have their post-high school help in the humanities through the junior college, or they have none. With the freshmen and sophomores, then, we have the greatest opportunity to influence the literary understanding of the great body of relatively intelligent, relatively cultured, relatively influential people, the people without whom a democracy cannot think sanely or act intelligently.

I have said that it is possible to teach literature to freshmen and sophomores. I now have to admit that literature is not always taught to these students. Sometimes even the catalogue admits that it is not taught; and so far as I may observe, more and more catalogues make this admission every year. Even where literature does appear in the catalogue, it is not always taught, for the teaching of literature is somewhat different from the teaching of most subjects, and not all pedagogues can teach it. One may teach chemistry, I suppose, without much imagination. Doubtless both the instructor and the instructed profit if imagination plays about the subject, but the main job is acquiring techniques and mastering a body of knowledge. If the knowledge is mastered and the skill acquired, the course is no failure. Similarly, a course in County and Municipal Government, or in Range Management, presumes the acquisition of a body of knowledge, knowledge which remains pretty much the same, whether the teacher has or has not an engaging personality. Not so in the teaching of literature, at least not to freshmen and sophomores. There is no body of knowledge to be taught. It makes no difference if the student knows Swift's patron's name or who Stella was. But whether Swift comes alive for the student, becomes a living, brooding personality through whom the wondering young man sees the eighteenth century taking shape like headlands beneath a clearing Aleutian fog; whether through Swift the young man comes to see what satire is and what it means for mankind that some sensitive souls strike out at all mankind because they hate stupidity, and cruelty, and greed; whether the student finds out what literature is—that matters very much.

─◀ 19. ▶─

The Devil, Teachers,
and World Literature

This piece was written at the invitation of the Comparative Literature Committee of the National Council of Teachers of English and was read at a national convention of that organization.

Being one who justifies his pay check in considerable measure by asking questions, and being aware that when I was to read this paper I should be among others who support their credit rating by this same irksome, not to say dubious practice, I was perturbed to discover evidence that the best examination questions have been asked by the Devil and his advocates. If it be true that the Devil is a professor at heart—even though, as I should trust, a professor who has missed his calling—this is indisputably a matter of some professional interest to all of us. How does it happen that the sons of darkness seem to ask better academic questions than the sons of light, among whom teachers are often fond of enrolling themselves? We might look at the evidence.

174

⟶⟨ Consider the primary catechism of mankind, that in which the Serpent asked the question and Eve gave the answer. This may properly be called The First Great Placement Examination, the ancestor of the SCAT Test, the ACT, and all the rest of them, for this was truly a placement examination. By her answer Eve determined that man should be placed outside, not inside, the Garden of Eden. You recall the occasion: the questioner was the Serpent, undoubtedly some embodiment of the Devil, and he may be said to have invented on this occasion that diabolical instrument known as the true-false examination. Jehovah, be it observed, when he questioned Adam had always asked what may be called thought-provoking questions. Not so, the Devil. He asked, in effect, "Oh yea" —I am merely adding *oh* to the King James version—"hath God said, Ye shall not eat of every tree of the garden?" True or false? This was obviously a leading as well as a supposedly objective question; Eve followed the lead, convinced Adam she had the right answer, and they both flunked the placement examination. Mankind has had his troubles outside the Garden ever since.

Before we continue to the next great examination, we might observe this one in somewhat more detail. We notice at once that the Serpent's query was not, *per se*, a notably good question. The timing at least as much as the question itself, produced the devastating impact. The time, the place, and the victim also are important, and just here, I suspect, lies the similarity between the Devil and the professor. If the Serpent had asked his question of an elm-tree beetle, for example, the insect would probably have replied, in the accent of a Freshman football aspirant, "Naw, jest elm trees," and would have gone about his hunt for an elm tree to eat. Since there is no record of there having been elm trees in the garden he would probably have maintained his uneasy innocence. But no. The Serpent asked his silly question at the exact time and of the

175

specific person so that it would flunk the human race, and I am reminded that this is just the complaint my students seem to have about me. I can pose a given question all semester with almost no perceptible result, but when I ask the question during an examination hour the slaughter is cataclysmic.

We might continue now to another significant catechism which can be appropriately denominated the Great Midterm Quiz. For brevity I am here passing over that preliminary quiz in which Satan, by the dexterously placed query, "Doth Job fear God for nought?" managed to needle Almighty powers into sanctioning Job's persecution, and thus raised the whole problem of good and evil. You recall the circumstances; Jesus was fasting in the Wilderness when the Devil asked him if he could not turn a stone into bread. This is what the students call a catch question, apparently easy, but having large implications. It elicited a straight-A answer, which was even given the color of having come out of the textbook: "It is written, That man shall not live by bread alone." Or consider the Great Final Examination, when Jesus stood before the Roman centurion, who may not have been the devil, but may plausibly be assumed to have been diabolically inspired. "What is truth?" Pontius Pilate asked, and even though the question was flippantly tossed off, and indisputably a good one, it was like many professorial questions, nothing new. It is certainly as old as curiosity itself, and the Greek philosophers had been propounding it for centuries and being answered mainly by the thunders of silence, if not indifference; but once the Devil through Pilate had asked the question of the right person at the right moment it could no longer be ignored. It has troubled the Western World ever since.

And how are we to answer these questions, if at all? Jesus, in asserting that his source declared that "man shall not live by bread alone," added the explanation, "but by every word of God." The reply is illuminating, so far as it goes, but at that point both the Lord and the Devil dropped the subject without going on to the next important question. Which of all the words in the world are the words of God? For this question, answers which are presumably divine seem frequently to be ambiguous also, and at best lacking in detail. Accordingly, man, under whatever auspices, has done much of the sifting of inspired from uninspired words, but when he has done so the answers have usually been characterized more by charming variety than by consistency. Even when individual groups of men have been able to agree that the Bible is the truth and the Koran is not, or that the tales told of Manabozo are the truth but the tales told of Thor and Woden are not, even the locally accepted truths are not accepted equally in all their parts. Presumably it is the truth, as Genesis assures us, that Peleg begat sons and daughters; there is no reason to doubt it, and the action was not unique with him, but most practicing Christians find less truth for them in the family life of Peleg than in the Lord's Prayer and the Sermon on the Mount. By man's definition truth seems not to be uniformly present even in truth.

What is truth, and how does man live by it? The bailiff in the court asks the witness to "tell the truth, the whole truth, and nothing but the truth." Of course no human has ever done this, and presumably none ever will; neither language nor the human mind suffices to tell the whole truth, not to mention the insistency urged on by what Andrew Marvell calls "time's winged chariot." The best words of man are but half-blind gropings into the eternal dark, but there has seldom been any doubt that some words or combinations of words contained more truth, or more useful truth, or more significant or more profound truth, than some other words, and I raise the question now because of the presistent feeling that the most telling human words are those which we call literature.

On the whole, man has gone about trying to find and tell the truth in two ways. Either he has tried to put together this inexplicable puzzle in which we live or he has assumed that it is together and he has endeavored to take it apart. The first we call art and the second science; of course neither of these exists much in pure form, and neither need be pure to be exciting or revealing, but on the whole the process of art is synthesis and the process of science analysis. Both have served man well.

Since I expect to say little of science, let us start with that. The aim of the scientist may be to produce a total, unified understanding, but he is likely to work by taking things apart rather than by putting them together. He divides phenomena into areas to which he gives such denominations as physics and chemistry, and he is likely to feel comfortable if he can study in one of these

areas, or one of the parts of them, and if he has to study the relationships between them he is likely to make an area of that. He then
fragments these areas; to take an ideal example one might observe
that the taxonomic botanist is not happy until he has divided the
plants of the world into classifications and sub-classifications and
sub-sub-classifications until each plant is distinct and its relationships described. Furthermore, the botanist is not content, or will not
be, until he has dissected each plant chemically as well as physically.
If the botanist ever gets this job done, presumably he could then
put the whole vegetable kingdom back together again, and leave it
as he found it except that it would be illumined with a valid and
comprehensive statement, but meanwhile he has worked mainly by
analysis and when synthesis has been possible he has been content
with minor syntheses based upon his main analyses.

As a matter of course I am offering no adverse comment on
the methods of the scientist; they are demonstrably valuable if
not uniquely so. I am endeavoring only to contrast the nature and
methods of the sciences with the nature and methods of the arts. The
artist is inclined to begin with a whole of sorts and try to envision
and build an even larger whole. He starts with a human being,
with an idea, with a theme, and the presumed result is a whole work
of art. True, he may use analysis in a secondary way, as the scientist uses synthesis after analysis; what is called "character analysis"
may be part of the activity of almost any artist, and with a work-
man like Henry James it may seem to become an obsession—in fact
it may become so much an obsession that little room remains for
synthesis—but even with an analytic person like James the analysis
is only preliminary to the finished work of art. A marine biologist
may feel he has finished his job when he analyzed the processes
by which a bit of seaweed extracts minerals from sea water, but
the artist does not feel he has finished his job until he has completed his novel, designed his ballet, or performed a sonata, each
of which is calculated to produce a total effect. Even as the artist
works he is likely to work with what seem to him wholes; he is likely
to explain that he has made a certain character act and speak in
a certain way because that is what that character would do in the
given circumstances, being the kind of person he is, not because

the analysis of the character shows him to be made up of certain parts.

Allowing, then, for the inadequacy of all brief generalizations, science and art seem to be characterized by two of the commonest mental processes, trying to understand by taking things apart and trying to understand by looking at wholes, that is, by analysis and synthesis. And what does all this have to do with the announced subject of this meeting, with the evaluation of methods for teaching world literature? I presume it has much to do with our subject partly because when we study art we are studying man and mankind. [For the development of this idea, see the previous lecture.] Thus, literature is the most meaningful of the arts because it uses as its medium language, and language provides a body of artistic symbols which is incomparably the most extensive and semantically the most nearly exact of any body of symbols used by any art.

But what about world literature? How does the study of world literature differ from the study of any other sort of literature? I should say that it is both the most rewarding and potentially the most dangerous, and that we ought to ask ourselves how far we are harvesting its rewards and avoiding its hazards. I assume that the virtue of studying literature is that we thereby study man through art; we study him as a whole, as intellect and emotion, as individual and society, as nature and experience, in every way that man is capable of conceiving himself. The danger is that we study literature not as art at all but as a phenomenon whose interesting trappings can be observed. Studied as art, world literature is notable for the extent to which it is representative and understandable; studied as the accumulation of a body of related data it offers few of the advantages of studying art. And of all bodies of literature what we call world literature most readily ceases to be the study of art and becomes the study of an agglomeration of related supposed fact.

In some ways, the more provincial the body of literature, the better. If the reader knows the time and place in which a novel is set, for example, and if the characters and the action are emotionally congenial to him, he can the more readily read the story as art, as crystallized distillation. Anyone who lived in one of the old brown-stone houses after it had become little better than a tenement must be able to read *Street Scene* as most of us cannot; the older generation can read *The Grapes of Wrath* with a ready participation denied to the generation born since the great depression, denied particularly to those who grow up with no sense of hunger, as most young Americans do today. As we recede from our experience, reading becomes harder and the appreciation of a written work of art more and more reliant upon a conscious reconstruction of a time and place we can never know. Shakespeare is written in English and is so vital that most of his plays can be enjoyed within limits by the uninitiated reader, but only within limits. In contrast, few modern readers can grasp any large part of what Dante's *Comedy* is about without extensive study of the man, the time, and the place. Furthermore, as soon as the reader gets far from his own language he faces the fact that written work can never be translated in any real sense, however indispensable translation may be, and this esentially alien quality in much of world literature grows from the diversity of time as well as culture. To most readers of English, *Beowulf* is as incomprehensible in the original as is the *Odyssey* and may require even more by way of translation and explication.

Of course this factually complicated character of the study of world literature has its compensations. As a sort of secondary reward, the study of world literature can become profitable as an intimate study of history, of geography, of society, of almost anything. The reader comes to know a good bit about thirteenth-century Florence, scholastic thought, and the medieval church before he is ever able to read the *Inferno* as a work of art. In fact, one suspects that many so-called courses in world literature have this virtue and this virtue only, that they become quite useful exercises in the pursuit of cultural history.

This is a virtue not to be despised; students are understandably intrigued to discover that Nausicaa is less shocked to observe that Odysseus was wearing no clothes than a nice American girl would have been, and they discover something about the nature of kingship in early Greece when they observe that the swineherd chats familiarly with his lord and master. These experiences are indisputably educational, but distinguishing which so-called kings are or are not more than tribal chiefs is not mainly our business as teachers of literature. That we teach something else under the title of literature would perhaps not matter greatly if we were not thereby failing to teach art in language at all, and I have endeavored to suggest that the teaching of the artistic comprehension of man seems to me one of the most deeply significant needs.

This is the great danger in teaching what is called literature, I suppose: that we never teach literature at all. Many a teacher has taught the names and dates of authors, the titles and the subjects of their works, the life and times in which the authors flourished, the facts of their lives, the circumstances of their copying or their publication, solemnized with well-chosen clichés of criticism, and has gone to his reward reassured by the belief that he has been teaching literature, whereas in fact he never suspected what literature is, to say nothing of having attempted to teach it. This teaching of something else other than literature under the name of literature is perhaps no more characteristic in our time of the teaching of world literature than of the teaching of some others sorts of literature. World literature has been saved in part by an emphasis upon what are called Great Books as against small snippets which have often been the bane of the teaching of survey courses in English and American literature.

But the danger is certainly most threatening in world literature. Here, by definition, the material of the subject constitutes the greatest works from the widest possible selection in time and space. The result is that the study of world literature profits from the greatest possible juxtapositions of the new and strange, but inevitably world literature requires the simple necessity of comprehension more by way of background and explication than does any other body of *belles lettres,* and the temptation is always to so multiply the trappings of literary study that the literature is obscured beneath the gay fringes of fact, the work of art ignored for the convoluted gilt frame in which it is set.

The teaching of world literature has, then, its dangers, the dangers inherent in the teaching of any literature, but dangers that are here at their most hazardous. Potentially, however, world literature is clearly the best body of material to teach, as literature.

If we are to assume that literature is the record of the best that man has thought and done, then in world literature we have the widest possible field from which that best can be chosen. Here is the whole range of human nature and human experience, of human need for expression and appreciation, and of artistic striving to satisfy that need. If creativity is the urge that has made man human, here in the chosen literature of the world is the richest accumulation of the wealth of man's intellectual and emotional life.

If what I have been saying is true then one corollary follows that concerns us here and now. If we are here to evaluate the teaching of world literature in our time then we must ask ourselves whether or not world literature is being taught. That is, is literature being taught under the title of the courses which are called world literature? This question is easy to ask, but not easy to answer. Finding out what happens in any course that one does not teach himself is extremely difficult; titles and even course descriptions are often not very revealing, and may be misleading, even deliberately so. I recall an example; I had the good fortune to take a course at Columbia University by the late Jefferson B. Fletcher called "Dante and Medieval Culture." This title would seem to promise a course in cultural history using at least some material from Dante's writings to illuminate his life and times. The course was anything but that; Professor Fletcher apparently believed, although he was no devotee of superlatives, that Dante had embodied man in his relation to man and man in his relation to God in an intricate artistic whole as no other human being had ever contrived to do, and he taught the *Comedy* as a great work of art. True, he knew thirteenth century history of Florence almost as though it were his own childhood; he knew and loved Dante's Italian; he moved easily in classical and scholastic thought, but when he drew upon this intricate background he did so to reveal Dante as a great artist in the use of language.

I recall his apologizing once for the title of the course. It seems that as a young man he had wanted to offer a course in Dante's *Comedy*, which he had studied under Grandgent at Harvard, but the Department of Italian objected. They, and only they were to teach Dante. The Department of History, however, was more broadminded, and did not object to the Department of Comparative Literature teaching cultural history in relationship to literature, and accordingly the powers fixed up a title which would keep everybody happy, while Fletcher went on teaching anything he pleased. Eventually with a change in personnel the attitude of the Department of Italian changed, but nobody bothered to change the catalogue, and consequently Fletcher continued for a quarter of a century teaching poetry under the name of cultural history.

Very little harm resulted, I should say, from this innocent academic hoax. Teaching poetry under the heading of history affected Fletcher's professorial performance not at all, but this, I suspect, is not the usual distortion. More frequently history is taught under the title of poetry, and I believe this does occasion a loss if thereby the literature never gets taught. And if we can seldom know whether or not our colleagues are teaching literature, we may have difficulty in knowing when we are teaching literature ourselves, particularly in a course inclusive enough to be called "world literature."

The troublesome fact is that literature is not easy to teach. Biographical fact, cultural fact, or political fact is often easy to apprehend and usually easy to transmit, but literary fact is uncommonly slippery stuff. Wholes are difficult to grasp and still more difficult to elucidate. Saying, "This is a poem—isn't it beautiful?" is not enough, although I fear that much supposed teaching of literature has not gone far beyond that level. Teaching literature well, like teaching anything else well, requires the teaching of fact. Furthermore, that literary fact is hard to grasp does not comprise the whole problem; in teaching literature, and especially in teaching any body of literature drawn from many times and diverse cultures, we must inevitably teach enough accompanying fact to make the work of art understandable in its time and place. The temptation, of course, is to teach the easy fact, the readily attractive facts that surround the work of art, and never teach the hard facts of what makes literature literature. Literature, especially world literature, is hard to grasp and hard to teach even if it is grasped.

I have no easy solution for this confused profession of ours. By its very nature I suspect that the problem admits of no easy solution and that solutions which appear easy seem so because if they are solutions at all they are solutions to something else, to a partial or peripheral problem, for example. The truth is that if we are to teach world literature well we must first know what literature is and we must then know what literature has been at various times and places. This must be the basis of our evaluation; if we do not know what literature is how can we teach what it is? In addition, we must be at least passably competent in a difficult technique, teaching the essence of literature in an area where the obscuring details are embarrassingly numerous.

If I have no simple solution, however, I can suggest a basis for evaluating what we do. We should be teaching fact as the basis of understanding, but when we teach it we should be leading into the written work as a work of art, not out of it toward biography, society, morals, philosophy, or anything else. This may not seem to you a very objective basis for measuring the worth of our teaching; I concede it is not, and I fear I am dubious about objective measurements in an area where the objectively determinable facts are likely to be the superficial facts. Literature is not superficial; it has its origin where man the animal becomes man the human being, and when we evaluate our teaching of world literature we must first ask, in the face of the great difficulty of teaching anything from a world point of view, are we teaching literature at all?

--◄ 20. ►--

A Do-It-Yourself Program
for Teaching Composition

The following excerpt comes from an article published
as cited below, under the title "Freshman English During
the Flood." It was based upon an experiment I conducted
at the University of Oregon at the invitation of the then
head of the Department of English, Philip W. Souers, who
was seeking a more economical way of teaching composition, particularly for the years when he feared he would
not be able to find competent teachers during the flood
of students resulting from the post-war baby boom. My
pilot classes led to a campus-wide experiment during the
following year, 1956–57.

College English, XVIII (1956), 131–38. Repr. Phi Delta Kap-
pan XXXVIII (1957), 204–210; College English Reprints, R-10
(1957).

--⚓ We started by asking ourselves what a section of freshman English costs in time. On the theory that a teacher with four sections of about twenty-five has a teaching load of at least forty-four hours a week, we assumed that teaching a section requires eleven hours, which we guessed might be spent about as follows: classes, three hours; correcting a set of papers, five hours; conferences, one hour; preparations, committees, staff meetings and the like, two hours. I determined to try to teach the section in a maximum of seven hours, budgeting my time about as follows: class, one hour; preparation, keeping class records, attending staff meetings, etc., one hour (pro-rated for one of four classes); reading papers and meeting individual students, two hours; group conferences (three students per conference, three conferences per hour), three hours. We assumed that if I could teach the class in seven or eight hours without worse results than I should have expected from eleven hours, we could theoretically increase an instructor's load twenty-five to thirty percent without either him or his class suffering appreciably.

My procedure was as follows. I told the class we would meet on Monday, but not as a class on Wednesday and Friday. Instead, they were to arrange themselves in groups of three (I later expanded this to four in most conference groups) to meet with me in conferences of fifteen minutes each, that is, in three sessions an hour with a little time for slack. I assigned a theme, which they were to bring with them to the conference.

At the conferences I explained the next step. The students were to correct one another's papers. Before the Friday class hour, each student was to read the paper he had received, suggest revisions by using the correction symbols in the handbook for the course, and write a considered statement of what was good and

186

what inadequate in the paper. At the class hour on Friday, the group was to convene in the regular classroom, or anywhere else that was convenient for them, and exchange papers again. Once more the students were to read the papers and recommend revisions, checking those suggested by the first critic, and adding any of their own, along with a written appraisal. Then each paper was to be returned to its author, and the students were to discuss the papers, endeavoring to clarify one another's criticisms. After this meeting the writer of the paper was to compose an estimate of the comments he had received, revise the paper in any way that now seemed fitting, and hand it to me in class the following Monday.

At that Monday meeting I assigned another theme, and prepared the students for the second round of writing and criticism by introducing a central subject for the week's study—relevance, significance, unity, or whatever. With the students embarked on their second paper, I prepared for my conference on the first set of papers, which I had just received. I wrote each student's name on a blank sheet of paper, clipped the sheets together in accordance with the conference groups, and used these sheets to keep a skeleton record of all the student's activities, in the theme and later in the conference. I read the set of themes rapidly, observing the comments made by the various critics, and especially the writer's rejoinder, noticed whether the revisions had been generally adequate, and took a few notes to refresh my memory. At the conference on Thursday I considered the three papers orally, reviewing the criticisms of the students and adding observations of my own. I resolved any differences of opinion, asked questions calculated to elicit specific evidence, and directed the comment toward the subject for the week, while seeing to it that each student was drawn into the discussion. For instance, I might say to A that I agreed that his critics had been right in their observations about this lack of unity, and I noticed that he had graciously accepted their animadversions, but I was curious to know what he would do another time to take advantage of these criticisms. In B's paper, both critics had objected to its being unclear, and in this they were probably right, but I doubted that they had found the best solution; I suspected that his topic sentences were at fault, and gave him examples. Each student received some comment on his paper and on his criticism of the other papers. Meanwhile, I completed the records I had started when I had read the paper, making jottings as we talked, including a grade for the theme, an observation on the student as a critic, his participation in the discussion, or anything that might be useful.

Since Monday the students had written their set of themes for that week. They exchanged them, received any special instructions pertinent to the revisions, and were dismissed. While they were being replaced by a second conference group, I filed their themes, laid out my new batch of corrected themes and record sheets, and was ready for my second conference. Now, this method of handling a section is simple and orderly enough, but since it involved simultaneous sequences for student and instructor, a skeletonized statement may be useful:

	Student	*Instructor*
Class meeting	Receives assignments, instructions, etc.	Assigns work for the week; collects theme from previous week.
Interim	Writes a theme.	Prepares for conference; reads themes from previous week; makes preliminary notes.
Conference	Exchanges week's theme with another student; receives instructions for criticizing; participates in conference.	Leads discussion of themes from previous week; completes records and files themes; gives instructions for reading current themes.
Interim	Reads and criticizes paper he has received.	Plays golf.
Student group meeting	Exchanges paper; reads second paper; receives own paper and participates in discussion of all papers.	Plays golf.

Interim	Writes estimate of criticisms he has received; revises theme.	Plays golf.
Class meeting	Returns corrected paper; receives instructions for the week.	Assigns work for the week; collects revised themes from previous week.

This process went on; each week a theme was written, criticized, revised, discussed, and filed by Thursday of the next week, by which time another theme was written and started on its cycle. In the one class meeting a week there remained some time for consideration of rhetorical principles, some *explications de texte*, but not much. At first, all of us were a bit confused, but after a few weeks the system was working smoothly. The students had learned to scrutinize writing, other people's writing and eventually their own, as they had never scrutinized any writing before. I was discovering that my job was no longer mainly criticizing students' work but showing students how to criticize one another's and their own work.

This procedure has obvious advantages, but we found some, also, which were not so obvious. The instructor saved time, as we had hoped he would. Since most of the commoner inelegances had been caught by one or another of the student critics, the instructor did not need to spend much time on routine correction. Deliberately, I cut the time for reading a set of papers to an hour, and found that I could acquire a passing notion of them in that time; when I increased the time to two hours it was quite adequate. We had predicted something of the sort, and we had predicted, also, some improvement in student attitude, but we were amazed at the improvement we observed. The whole level of the class rose, and the better students became downright enthusiastic. I would receive reports of how they met and argued about their papers by the hour, and about the form and adequacy as well as the content. Both the mechanics and the rhetoric improved. As one young man put it, "When you've said that something the other guy has done is lousy, you better be careful not to do it yourself." No longer did students glance at the grade on a theme, make a few revisions which might or might not be improvements, return the paper, and forget the whole bothersome business. One student explained the difference in this way: "If the teacher marks something wrong on your paper, you think probably he knows, and you don't do much about it. But if a student marks your paper, you think maybe he's wrong and you can catch him at it, so you look it up." Another said that in trying to prove he was right he had learned a lot of rules he didn't know were in the book; checking the themes he had submitted during the previous term revealed that these statements had been called repeatedly to his supposed attention.

Numerous side advantages appeared. There were few late papers, usually only for illness. Plagiarism vanished. He would be a foolhardy student who would submit work not his own, knowing it was to receive the scrutiny and the public discussion for which it was destined, and I found that the students were much more rigorous in rebuking tendencies toward shady practice than I would have been—or at least enough of them were—partly because they had sure grounds for their suspicions. Tension between teacher and student lessened; the student now felt he knew the teacher as a human being, and the teacher was no longer his severest critic. The student found, on the whole, that his contemporaries did not much admire his prose, but that the teacher could usually find at least something good in it, or at worst would show him how to improve it. The comments written by the student critics tended to force the student to decide what he wanted to say; incidentally these bits of impromptu criticism provided the teacher with material he had wanted but did not usually get—samples of the student's writing which were not fixed up because they were "themes." When the student who had triumphantly caught his colleague misspelling *too* then had misspelled the same word twice in his critical comment, he was prepared to take seriously the instructor's suggestion that he should watch all his writing more carefully.

The procedure works, I believe, because the student receives less instruction in *writing* but more help in *learning to write*, and because he is in better state to learn. He spends relatively little time in classes where a few students are trying to show off, a few others are trying to keep from being called on, and a good many are a little drowsy and greatly bored. Nobody can gaze dreamily out the window during a conference group, not if the instructor does his job. Furthermore, each student is personally concerned, and can be made to feel personally concerned, with every paper taken up in the conference group. Either he has written it, or he has criticized it, and he is personally responsible for any ineptitudes that remain undetected, for any weakness not already observed in the papers written by the other students as well as those in his own composition. He is now writing for somebody, for at least two fellow students as well as the instructor, and he knows that they are likely to respond vigorously to what he writes. As a result, he is both more stimulated and more chastened. The student feels that he is learning something, and he is the readier to learn. Besides, he is having fun.

Of course there are dangers and difficulties. Students, for example, are skillful mimics, and an inadequate student who wishes to escape embarrassment will quickly learn to write, "This is a good paper, John. It is well organized, and you make your points well, but you need to watch your sentence structure. Some of the sentences are not very clear." Of course the instructor can combat this sort of thing, and exposing imitative generalities soon becomes one of his major concerns. He can point out that these statements mean little without evidence, and what is the evidence? Still better, he can ask John if he knew what the criticism meant, and if not, why did he not ask the critic what it meant? What is good about the organization and bad about the sentences? The principle must be established early, and made to work, that a student can be pardonably uncertain as to what to praise and what to blame, but that failing to ask himself questions and then writing windy nonsense is outside the pale.

Perhaps the principal weakness in the system as I have described it appears in the meeting of students which is not attended by the instructor. When enthusiasm is high students go to this meeting zealously, but control is uncertain there, although the instructor may manage a sort of remote control by turning conference discussions to a review of the talk in the student group meeting. Professor John Sherwood has tried a variation upon the general plan which provides for a supervised meeting, during which the students read and revise one another's papers. The instructor is present in the room, but available only for consultation. The students criticize in groups during this class session, but do not criticize one another's papers outside this meeting. This variation provides for much less revising by the students, lacks the spontaneity of at least some meetings which students hold with each other, and is, I should say, not so good for the better students. It is safer if the instructor is aiming at a reasonable minimum of revision, and is probably to be preferred if the instructor feels uncertain of his hold upon the class, or fears he has a relatively irresponsible group of students. [In subsequent experiments I increased my control by having group conferences of four, and requiring the students in rotation to write a report of the meeting, which became one student's theme for that week. This device worked very well.]

If the system does not cure student irresponsibility, it aggravates the consequences, and it may do either. Any laxity in attending the group meeting or in preparing papers on time or passing themes is uncommonly troublesome to the collaborative groups, since a shiftless student can cause his fellow students considerable inconvenience. Faculty members have long ago become inured to the nuisance students cause by being irresponsible, but students tend to be delicate creatures, not yet accustomed to the nuisance they can cause one another.

Some difficulties are certain to appear when the method is tried on a large scale. It requires office space, and teaching assistants who sometimes find themselves herded into large rooms may have difficulty obtaining privacy enough for group conferences. On the other hand, the system has many administrative adaptations. It would permit larger use of classrooms on Tuesday and Thursday, since a three-credit course does not meet at the scheduled hour three times a week. It permits an instructor to juggle his sections so that he can get whole days free, or mornings or afternoons free, either to concentrate or distribute appointments as he chooses. Some administrators hope that the system will render freshman English obsolete as a course and will permit substituting instead a standard of competence to be attained, whether in three months or three years. The students would undergo some formal indoctrination, either by large lectures or through sections, from which they would proceed into collaborative groups like those described, where they would receive help so long as they want or need it.

Some supposed difficulties are more apparent than real. We were all disturbed a little at first by the fact that much of the student criticism was not well done, and that accordingly, from an objective point of view, a paper is not so well corrected by this system as it would be if a competent teacher were to spend ten minutes or more on it. This reservation stemmed from the time when we assumed that a student learns mainly from being "corrected." We soon observed however, that the student learned from criticizing other people's papers, and from the fact that his inadequacies, when they came to light, became so much his personal business that he did something about them. As director of students' collaborative efforts I soon learned not to worry too much about individual lapses in correction, but to be much concerned about the general approach to correction and improvement, confident that any important matter would be picked up fairly soon. And I learned that the instructor can occasion considerable alertness by remarking, "Mr. Smith, I notice a vague pronoun in the last sentence of your second paragraph, although to my surprise neither Miss Jones nor Mr. Davis seems to have caught it. The sentence reads as follows . . ."

In short, those of us who have been associated with the experiment at the University of Oregon thus far are convinced that we have developed workable devices for the teaching of composition. Naturally, there is diversity of opinion as to which parts of the experiment have been most successful, as to which methods are most advisable, as to how valuable the approach may be, but all who have taught the system agree that they found unusual and unexpected advantages in the use of collaborative groups, and these teachers include some who were deliberately chosen because they were the most outspoken critics of the method when it was first proposed.

[At this point the original included more detailed discussion of the various steps in the method, and further discussion of its virtues and limitations; see the citations above. Results of the campus-wide experiment the following year were reported by

Professor John C. Sherwood, who directed it; see *Final Report: Composition Experiment* (University of Oregon, n.d., repr. *College Composition and Communication*, X, 1958). An extensive testing program provided by the Ford Foundation demonstrated that the approach using collaborative student groups did indeed improve composition more than did the more usual approaches, and that students taught through such groups improved even more in reading than they did in writing. I also conducted some further trials, using teaching assistants and adapting the method to both remedial and advanced students. I found that when properly used it helped with all grades of students and all sorts of instructors; so far as I know it has not been used in the secondary schools, but I am convinced it could be. It has been tried, also, on some other campuses. In rare instances it has been unsuccessful, I am convinced only because the instructor did not learn to adapt his teaching to a method as yet foreign to him. If a teacher insists on lecturing at his students, he might as well lecture at big groups as little ones. If he thinks of his duty as ramming unwelcome truth down resisting throats he will not be able to use the collaborative group method. He has to become convinced, and to implement his conviction, that he will teach best by submerging himself and by inducing students to teach themselves by trying to teach one another.]

-◄ 21. ►-

Language:
Ideas that Have Helped Teachers

Many readers will want to skip this chapter; its contents can all be found elsewhere in the lectures. On the other hand, I have found that in meetings teachers welcomed having these ideas brought together, and I suspect that some will be glad to have them printed together. The statement has been read to several teachers' groups but has not been printed in this form.

–◄ Recently, I conducted courses in Portland, Oregon, at the joint invitation of the Portland School Board and the Ford Foundation, whereby courses were part of a summer institute intended to improve the content of high school English teaching. My portion of the institute mainly concerned language, and since I had the opportunity to talk the second summer to teachers who had been my students the first summer, I gained some evidence as to what had been useful. To my surprise I seemed to have done more good with ideas the teachers could use for their own morale and for their convictions as to what they were doing and why, than with ideas they could use with their students, although there were some of the latter, also. Naturally, there was overlapping; teachers bubbling with ideas inevitably set students to effervescing, also.

The following are the ideas that seemed to help teachers most:

1. *Language is a continuing miracle, exciting in itself, worth teaching for itself.* Fortunately, knowing about it is fun, and we can teach it for itself. We may doubt that we can teach much usage; we may be uncertain, when we correct young people's English, whether we are harming their egos more than we are helping their social stations, but when we teach language we can be sure we are teaching a continuing good. Anyone who will become excited about language and stay excited about it will grow in his command of it. And language has mainly to be grown. It cannot be gulped down like nauseous medicine. It must be lived with, and it works best if the student has fun with it while he lives with it.

2. *There is no such thing as the grammar of English, or for that matter, of any language.* The grammatical statement you end with depends upon the grammatical assumptions you start with. No known language relies upon only one grammatical principle,

and when principles conflict, which will the grammarian prefer? He must prefer one, and distort his grammatical statement accordingly, while a grammarian of a different persuasion will prefer another principle, and distort in another direction. Actually, the choices are more pervading than this contrast suggests, because the emphases change as one's assumptions change; for example, English clearly makes use of function, structure, meaning, and a good many other grammatical devices, but none of these has been exactly defined. Every grammarian endeavors to construct a somewhat systematic statement about the working of a language, but any statement will be colored by the fact that it grows from assumptions which cannot be objectively evaluated, and any individual grammatical statement will be colored by the individual who prepares the statement. Even supposedly objective sciences are not objective; biologists cannot tell whether some substances are living or dead, and grammar, at least in the present state of our knowledge, if it is a science at all is not a very objective science. There is no simple right and simple wrong in grammar.

3. *Grammatical understanding is a real and important thing.* Careful examination of a language will suggest the way it works, and a knowledge of the working of language helps both an understanding and a command of language. No one grammar may be exclusively right, and more than one grammar may be useful. The most detailed grammar, the most objective grammar, the most significant grammar may or may not be the most useful grammar. Furthermore, the teaching of the language to native speakers may present quite different problems from those raised in teaching English as a second language. Personally I am guessing that in spite of its lack of objectivity, teaching functions will continue to be useful in helping young people grow to a command of English.

4. *Recent grammatical study, although it may be revolutionary, need not be confusing.* By now everybody concerned with grammar and everybody alert to modern thought about language knows that the conventional grammatical statement taught in the schools is to a degree erroneous and to a much larger degree inadequate. Meanwhile, new grammatical approaches have arisen which use new terminology, new assumptions, and produce seemingly heterodox conclusions. Facing this confusion and seeming

contradiction, many serious teachers have despaired; when the doctors disagree, what can one do about the dying patient? The situation is not so serious as this analogy suggests, in fact; not serious at all. New examinations of language from new points of view have produced new evidence, much of it very useful, useful even to the practicing teacher who remembers that he has to face Mary and Johnny tomorrow, whatever the doctors are arguing about. First, although the conventional parts of speech are harder to defend than they used to be, the conventional concept of function is not very far from the concepts on which most grammarians rely. Second, much of what the newer grammarians have revealed is knowable and teachable within the familiar concepts like those involved in the subject-verb-complement pattern, plus such other hardy perennials as subordination and coordination.

5. *Philosophically, standards and usage present no problems.* Even though language lives and grows by use, the people make it what they want it to be, and should so make it; however they do this, what they make is by definition right. They always want stability, more stability than they can ever get, and accordingly we have every right to endeavor to teach stability in usage. Actually usage may be difficult to determine, and it is always difficult to standardize, but we have ample authority to teach usage, if we can find out what it is.

6. *Teachers must teach usage, but they can never hope to teach much.* Language rests upon use, and "usage" may be thought of as that part of the question of use which concerns those locutions which are or are not approved by the community. Obviously, usage can be important socially, financially, personally, and in almost every way that involves daily living. It has little linguistic importance, but this is clearly one area in which linguistics must be subservient to practical social fact. People get jobs and lose them and get wives or divorce them by the use of language, including usage in language. A teacher can teach some of it to students who want to be taught, but he can never teach much, particularly to those who do not want to learn it. Little Billy, who learned to say *he don't* from his practical-minded father and his illiterate mother, who wants to do nothing but get big enough to work in a filling station, who hears *he don't* all day long from his family and friends and hears *he doesn't* one hour from his teacher,

will go right on saying *he don't* no matter how much of his precious time the English teacher wastes trying to teach Billy what he does not want and does not much need.

7. *One of the main jobs is to teach adult sentence patterns.* Simple English sentence structure is easy, so easy that children master it during preschool years. But adult sentence structure is extremely complex, and most people never learn to handle it with any facility. Johnny can't read or write either, partly because he has never learned adult sentence patterns. How can he learn them? In many ways, but in a literate society perhaps he can learn most readily by extensive reading of literate prose. Many pupils today never learn to command the language in any real sense because they read simplified textbooks and writing on a comic-book level and little else. Most students can be expected to develop extensive command of adult English only if they are kept in the presence of adult sentence patterns so that they can learn them naturally as they learned elementary English naturally.

8. *The native language should be taught as the vital thing it is.* Many a well-meaning English teacher spends hours teaching the diagramming of sentences to reveal parts of speech which cannot be defined as the diagrammer is endeavoring to use them, to reveal a grammar which is not there. They labor to teach youngsters not to put prepositions at the ends of sentences, whereas every good writer has to put so-called prepositions at the ends of sentences and every student of language knows it. Meanwhile, these teachers never tell the student that writing and speaking are using the language to say something, that writing which says nothing is bad writing however "correct" it may be. The great crime in English is not putting prepositions at the ends of sentences; it is presuming to use the language to say nothing. But we teachers are not alone in our too-frequent triviality. Many a parent corrects Johnny's supposed "bad grammar," but he is a rare father or mother indeed who rebukes Johnny for not having anything to say and for not using language vigorously to say it.

The following are among the useful ideas that teachers can use with students:

1. Students should be taught to use language, not merely to dissect it. Notably, they should be taught to choose sub-

jects, and on the whole they are not being taught. They should learn how to use rather than misuse the passive voice and the expletives, and how to put expressive verbs to work.

2. Students can be taught sentence patterns by a variety of devices, among them the use of nonsense syllables.

3. Etymology, particularly the concept of language families and the use of Indo-European bases, makes exciting study. For this the teacher needs some background, but summaries in semipopular books on language and in the introductions to dictionaries can provide the necessary insight.

4. Much the same thing can be said of semantic change; young people are excited to discover that one word can, in effect, become hundreds, and are intrigued by the processes of mind that have led to the growth and life of words.

5. Something rather similar is true for General Semantics, the Hayakawa sort of thing; this is, of course, pretty well known and rather widely used now.

6. Linguistic geography and dialect study generally provide exciting means of teaching usage. This is one area in which students can embark on studies themselves, and do a sort of research in their own communities.

7. Names can be fun, and any map or telephone directory gives youngsters a place to start.

8. The study of dictionaries can stimulate young people. Students can compare dictionaries, finding out how they are made, and even make their own, and can learn a good bit about language in the process.

A Few Tricks of the Trade,
Especially Concerning Examinations

The following miscellany has not been delivered as a lecture; it is a catchall of the sort of thing I recall saying during discussions at teachers' meetings.

Anyone who has read a considerable number of the preceding lectures will be aware that I place relatively little reliance upon methods and methodology. There are exceptions; obviously methods are important in dealing with small children, and some methods are better than some others for various subjects, ages, and circumstances. During the Middle Ages, the university professor lectured perforce; printed books were not available, and writing materials were expensive. The modern research worker or specialist may find himself in much the same situation; what he has to say is too recent to have found its way into print, at least in the form in which he wishes to organize it, and accordingly there is not much he can do but lecture, while his students take notes. With modern mass media, including that greatest of all audio-visual devices, the book, lecturing is obviously an awkward and uneconomical way to teach most material, and many teachers have done too much of it. But methods cannot make teachers; they can only help teachers to develop. Good teachers are good because they have brains, great learning, engaging personalities, deep devotion to teaching, and enough experience to learn what to do with themselves.

Good approaches can help, however, and the following are some which I have found useful and which seem to have interested teachers when I have described them.

First, a teacher should ask himself very seriously what he is trying to do in a course, what are his immediate objectives and what his ultimate aims. I assume I have suggested in the lectures above what I believe some of the aims should be, but I have said nothing about how these aims should be reflected in examinations, which are extremely important because here, as usually nowhere else, the teacher can tell students what he is trying to do in a way that the young will understand. The teacher should consider both the purposes of the examination, which should reflect the purposes of the course, and the means by which the examination can be adapted to the subject and to the students involved.

Of course teachers could live more honest and probably more revealing lives if there were no such things as grades or credits, at least not while the student is in attendance. I could imagine an ideal school system—at least for all but very small children— in which the student would be politely dismissed after a number of years, and told to return in five years if he wanted grades and credit. On his return he would be asked to produce evidence of use he had made of the course, its content, and its effect upon his life. If he had to admit that he could recall very little from the course and could not remember ever trying to use it, he should be failed. On the other hand, assume that he says something like the following: "You know that little two-credit course in geology I took? I've had fun with that ever since. Whenever I travel I can see geology all over; I can spot nonconformities in a mountainside, and old hanging valleys, and standing at a curb once I found myself staring a trilobite in the face. I was glad to see an old friend; I knew him when. I even used geology in my business a little. Knowing about it has helped me understand about how land lies and how population is likely to adapt to it, and where we should locate a new branch." That student should obviously get an A in geology. He would probably get an A in his course in literature, also, but if upon examination it is found that he has not tried to read a serious book outside his immediate professional or technical concerns, he should be failed in any courses he has taken in literature.

But grades and credits we have with us, and our school systems being what they are and American society what it is, we are likely to have them for some time. Since we must use them, we may as well use them to advantage, to promote what the teacher believes to be important. They should not be used—as many are —to divert the student's attention toward trivia. After all, students in an examination are usually emotionally stimulated; they are likely to be in an excellent state to learn, so that the teacher may be able to do more teaching in one hour than he can usually manage in a week.

First, the teacher will do well to recognize that there is no such thing as an objective examination, although I am aware that in making this statement I am defying much learned opinion. All examinations are made by somebody, or a committee of some-bodies, and they reflect the prejudices, preferences, and peculiarities of those who drafted the examination. Furthermore, of two students who give the "wrong" answer, one may be wrong because he knows too little, and the other wrong because he knows too much—too much for the examination, that is—and has seen implications that the author of the examination had not noticed. I recall the now-famous question, "What is the opposite of unless?" The only "correct" answer allowed by the answer sheet was *although*, but a perceptive student would probably conclude, after spending more than the allotted time, that there is no antonym of *unless*.

Of course objectivity is a desideratim and should be cultivated, but I find I can do a better job if I frankly admit to myself and to the students that I would only be bemusing myself and them if I pretend I can be objective. I use all the evidence I can bring to bear when I give a grade, but I do not assume that the same answer provides the same evidence for any two students. I try to think myself into the student and his future and ask myself what of genuine consequence, if anything, he seems to have gotten out of the course, and I at least color my grade accordingly. Usually in any but highly specialized courses I do not fail a student who has made an industrious and honest effort, even though a bad one, but I also ask what he, as a human being, has done about the experience I tried to provide him.

An examination will inevitably have more than one effect and it should have more than one purpose. An examination may provide a final grade, and in very large classes a teacher may have to accept this as the main purpose of the examination; of course there should never be any classes that large, without conference sections, but that is another matter. For this limited purpose the so-called "objective" examinations are handy; they look authoritative, they are usually accepted gullibly by the students. They can be graded by unskilled labor, and slightly doctored they can be used year after year. Unfortunately, unless they are very skillfully drawn—and usually they are not—they tend to test little that is much worth teaching, and they encourage the student to believe that the course concerns a large number of minor details that he need only to commit to memory. The worst, of course, are the true-false examinations; the best that I have tried are the multiple-choice questions, if they are so drawn that they require thinking and are directed toward the important aims of the course. Personally I believe in the essay question varied with the short answer question; I believe in writing and in forcing students to write. The difficulty for the teacher is that the papers must be read, which takes time. I have never found that good teaching is either quick or easy, although in school systems that overload the teachers an individual may or may not be able to do anything about that. In drafting an examination the teacher should recognize that not all minds are the same or work in the same ways, and that if time permits, several sorts of questions should be used in each examination, some more philosophic, some more objective.

The teacher should use every examination as much for pedagogical purposes and as little for measuring purposes as the circumstances will allow. If the class is of moderate size the teacher should know the students so well by the end of a term or a semester or a year or whatever, that he needs to rely but little on a final examination to assign a grade. This gives him a chance to encourage a thoughtful review, to induce the student to evaluate what he has learned, and the like. Many approaches can be used to encourage such results; here are two I have tried. I offer the class an option; they are to think the course through, and in a dozen or fifteen questions to embody their convictions as to the most important ideas and content in the course. If their questions are good enough I will mark one or more of these questions, which will become that individual student's examination; the student will have written his own examination. If the questions are not good enough, not hard enough, or omit important matters in the course, I will give the student questions, hard questions, and particularly questions covering the parts of the course that have been neglected. This seems to most of the students such a good bargain that they set out upon a genuinely industrious and thoughtful review. If they do not, of course, and they are faced with my questions, they

206 • A Few Tricks of the Trade

have only themselves to blame. In a variation upon this I offer to receive outlines of the course, with discussions of its aims and purposes. If these are good enough, I will accept them in lieu of an examination, from which the student will be excused.

Now for some offbeat teaching methods. The first I worked out in connection with a general introductory language course, although it could be applied in some other subjects as well. I adopt no text, but ask the students to pick up a packet of paperbacks in which I have included a combination of cheap reprints. Since standard things like Susanne K. Langer, *Philosophy in a New Key*, Joshua Whatmough, *Language*, and Edward Sapir, *Language*, can be had for prices ranging from fifty cents up, I can get quite a collection for eight or ten dollars. In secondary schools where the textbooks are supplied by the school system there may be complications, but teachers tell me they are able to do something—buy a collection of paperbacks with a number of duplicates for the library, for instance.

At the first meeting of the class I say that our responsibility for the term is to ask the most significant questions we can about language and to find answers if possible; the students are not only to provide the answers, they are also to ask the questions, in effect to outline the course; how would they like to begin? I make only three reservations; the students must agree upon something to do for the next day, and to continue planning ahead; they must themselves endeavor to find the answer to any question they raise before they consult any published treatment; and in the interests of a balanced coverage, I reserve the right to terminate any line of pursuit if it threatens to preempt the whole course, leaving other areas unexamined. And now, who has an idea of how we might start?

At first this staggers the students. In spite of all that we as teachers and citizens have heard about students wishing to run courses and to be allowed to do more original work, most of those who come to me want to be told and they do not want to be made to think and to take responsibility. But the better ones will rise to the occasion, the others will come along, and eventually most of the students welcome the opportunity.

I solicit suggestions, helping the students to refine these, volunteering only when I have to. Usually one or all of three suggestions are made: that we try to define language, try to find out its origin, or study something about semantics—since some of the students will have read Hayakawa in high school. I suggest that for the first, language is hard to define and the project not very fruitful anyhow because we all know what language is. It is the stuff we are using right now. But does anybody care to propose a concrete way to go at defining it? If nothing comes of that, we may turn to the second, the origin of language. I insist upon a means of procedure and when questioned I admit that nobody has ever been able to discover the origin of language. I add that the English language can be traced back to Indo-European, or Indo-Hittite, or something, and how is their Hittite? If no one else makes the proposal I eventually remark that they might revise the suggestion into something about the growth of language.

In this way we work toward some feasible project. Since a number of students will have heard that English has been borrowed from French, with a little help from the instructor if necessary, we may get a project something like the following. Every student will open his desk dictionary at random and check the etymologies of the next fifty words, putting the native words in one column and the borrowed words in another column, and study the results. Every student is to compose a written one-sentence statement of his conclusions, and be prepared to defend these conclusions with evidence. Some youngster is likely to notice that the borrowed words are longer than the native words, that they tend to be more general, or more technical. Each student then checks such hypotheses against his own list and tries to generate new hypotheses. This investigation can well lead to a more specific one; for example, each student may write down the first twenty-five words that come to his mind about some subject that interests him, law and the courts, dressmaking, hockey, or whatever. Or he may write down the names of objects in a room, or visible out the window. Students will find that words like *eat, bread, cook,* and *drink* are native words but that *delicatessen, roulade,* and *Hassenpfeffer* are all borrowed. Within a very short time the class can work out fundamental principles concerning language borrowing, semantic change, the relationships between language and society, language and thought, and the like. Furthermore, every student can be made to see that he could have worked out these principles himself if he had studied his own evidence carefully enough.

Once this sort of thing is started it builds up rapidly. Students will discover dozens of projects and the instructor may have to exercise his option of stopping a subject like semantics and going on to phonology or grammar, but by this time projects will have appeared in those areas as well. And occasionally, if the instructor wants to encourage a review in preparation for a quiz, or if he needs a few classes to lecture about a subject too difficult for the students to do much with, he can suggest that the class take a week or so to go at the books and see if anybody has been able to discover anything about the subject that the class has not found out.

Like most methods, this one has its dangers and its virtues. It is not an easy way to teach; the teacher must know something. He cannot hope to teach by reading a textbook and keeping two assignments ahead of the class; he cannot hope to survive with lectures prudently saved from last year, or written out by cribbing reference works or refurbishing old class notes. The method also requires that the teacher do some thinking; he cannot just blindly follow a textbook. For example, he had better have some good projects in the back of his head so that if the class flounders hopelessly—and sometimes they will—he can step in and save things. Particularly, he had better have some workable projects for that first assignment, which he can hint at if necessary.

On the other hand, a method like this promotes exciting teaching; some students are sure to take ideas and run with them, and discover much more about themselves and the nature of truth and of learning than could ever be taught by the conventional sequence of lecture and assignment, assignment and lecture. With this sort of approach, when the instructor does find himself lecturing, he is talking because the students want something that they have not been able to get from any other source, and when the students themselves go to their books, they are not just reading pp. 83–97; they are hunting for information, and they are reading with some critical evaluation.

A somewhat similar method, which I have been inclined to

use as one of several approaches within various courses on literature, relies upon student panels. I organize the students into small groups, say about five to a panel, or preferably get them to organize themselves. I then propound a number of questions or subjects. For a junior college course I may offer a number of novels, with the possibility of my approving almost any other proposal from a student that makes any sense at all, and ask each panel to make this novel the center of their study. For a more advanced class I might ask by what means did the sonnet go to England or how one can account for the great increase in serious prose in the seventeenth century. After a period in which the panel is given time to make a tolerably serious investigation of the subject, they are given a class period or two in which they appear before the class.

The period will be mainly discussion, with the remainder of the class asking questions. The panel may plan their presentation; this may include brief statements by various members, but I will not tolerate rambling reports, digested from encyclopedias and read out to everybody's boredom. The panel must study the subject seriously, although they may designate certain members to specialize, one to read the available biographies of the author, another to canvass the critical reception of the book, and the like. I ask questions of the panel only if the other students will not ask enough questions or questions that are searching enough. Usually I have little to do except to see that the ground rules are enforced, that no panelist is allowed to fill up the time by reading out prepared summaries of conventional pronouncements he has never made his own. The students may be baffled at first; they will have become accustomed to giving reports that have been little more than digests of reference works, but once they have discovered that they are supposed to be trying to find out the truth in an uncertain world, and they are working together at problems too big for them, the class is likely to take fire.

Part of the secret of both these approaches, of course, is that the student is encouraged to teach himself, partly by inducing him to face the problems of the world as they apply to him. A variation on these approaches can be used to induce the student to consider the principles of literary art as experience. Here I require that each student try to write each sort of genre before we start studying it. I start with relatively brief, simple forms like the haiku or the ballad, and go on to the more complex genre. Of course I cannot expect every student to write a novel before we start studying novels, but he can write a brief prospectus of a novel and attempt to write a single scene or a few paragraphs. Some of the best efforts are read in class or distributed in dittoed form, and these become the basis for discussing what the writers were trying to do. From these attempts we go on to observing how professional writers have faced the same problems, although the professionals were both more skillful and more penetrating in the solutions they devised. In this the purpose is not to produce good creative writing—although that is of course welcome when it occurs —but to involve the student in creativity, in what it is and what it does to people.

Obviously a little ingenuity will devise variations upon such approaches, adaptations to various age levels, or new methods having similar aims. Personally, I like teaching of this sort because I find it recreative for the teacher, because it promotes good results with the students, and because I can believe it is honest teaching. The word *honest* here may puzzle many teachers; they have not themselves made a practice of pilfering purses, and with good reason they have believed that they are uncommonly concerned with honesty at all levels. To them I can say only that I was myself a teacher of many years' experience before it occurred to me that I had been engaged unconsciously in a sort of essential dishonesty. True, I had never said in so many words to my students: "You are born into a well-ordered world, an essentially benevolent and understandable world, where truth is certainly and rather easily apprehended, where all you need to do is to read the right books and listen to the right teachers, to behave yourselves and do what you are told." I had not told them that, but I knew that they believed something of that sort, and I had not spent much time insisting to them, "Behold, we know not anything." And even if I had said something of the sort, in general, I had gone on teaching as though I did not believe it, and I had never handled my classes in such a way that the vastness of our ignorance or the inadequacy of our grasp would have become a working sense in most of my students.

Within limits, of course, the young must be shielded from the truth. A baby must believe that his mother can protect him against anything; a small child trusts that his father is the most powerful creature in existence, and that the sun and the moon follow each toddler around, that the world exists for him. Such simple ethnocentrism does not last long, but it is likely to be replaced by a school and home life which provides rewards for the limited virtues of docility, obedience, and promptness, and not much for the larger virtues of questioning everything and everybody, of demanding evidence as a prerequisite to belief, of stubbornly insisting upon trying something new if anything new can be found to try. Of course this is what the educative process is in any larger sense; acquiring skills and facts and explanations is only a lesser part of education. Education is learning to control and develop the mind, learning to outgrow the limitations that the fears and bigotry and provincialism of childhood encourage in us. But much so-called education is not education in any real sense, not much more than a sort of intellectual and social toilet training. I may not be able to teach anything more than that, but I like to believe I am trying.

—◄ 23. ►—

Auctorial Cohabitation:
Authors and Their Editors

This lecture concerns the writing likely to be done by teachers more than the writing they are likely to teach, but I include it as a sort of grace note since I trust it answers some of the questions most frequently raised at teachers' institutes, and that writing a textbook is a little like matrimony, it goes better if one enters into it for the right reasons and the contracting parties understand one another's motives. The piece was written at the invitation of Professor J. N. Hook and read at the 1966 convention of the National Council of Teachers of English in Houston.

Publishers and English Teachers: Allies in Education (Champaign, Ill.: National Council of Teachers of English, 1967), pp. 9–14

⟶◀§ I have been asked to reveal the secrets whereby, as the result of intercourse between a writer and the publisher's representatives, a book is born. Our mutual friend, Nick Hook, when he invited me to consider this subject, indicated that if I was too lazy to do any thinking I could just reminisce—though I should add that he was much too kind to phrase the proposal in this way. I shall take advantage of his genial offer, partly because I know my own experiences better than I know the troubles of others, but since this should be a serious consideration of what is, for many teachers, a serious problem, I shall try also to analyze.

First we should recognize that there are authors and authors, editors and editors, and a great variety of books; nothing one can say will fit all these, either books or human beings, but we may notice some trends. One reads accounts of the printer's devil sitting on Dickens' doorstep, waiting for the next installment of a novel in order to scurry to the printer who would set the installment into type. In fact, the common notion of the creative process is that somebody who can write gets an idea, fumes and scribbles and squabbles with his wife—or husband—about it, gets pleasantly drunk, and stays that way for months while the manuscript becomes somehow completed; the publisher accepts it with delight, and prints, after which both author and publisher roll in wealth. If this Auctorial Nirvana ever existed, I assume it exists no more. The later Hemingway is said to have sent manuscripts to his publisher with the admonition that if so much as a comma was changed he would place the manuscript with another publisher; I presume one can do that, if he is a later Hemingway, but all readers of Maxwell Perkins' autobiography know that most writers, even most of the Hemingways—whether young, middle, or aging—recognize that editors can be useful. On the whole, however, serious creative writers

213

probably use editors less than do most authors. I doubt that any editor greatly altered many of Robert Frost's poems.

At the other extreme are the great reference works, which can come into being only through the complicated and continued interaction of the author and representatives of the publisher. Who can imagine the *Encyclopaedia Brittanica* being written in a garret and, after delivery from a furniture van, inundating the editor's desk? A cooperative reference work which has borne the working title of *Guide for Comparative Literature,* with which the NCTE has been associated, provides a case in point. The late Arthur E. Christy conceived an annotated bibliography for the comparative study of literature and talked a foundation into paying for the clerical help and a publisher into assuring publication. A staff was developed including some two hundred specialists as contributors, sub-section editors, section editors, and a general editor, and for the publisher, an editor with his assistants. When Professor Christy died the whole came to a halt. Revived, it came to another halt when the publisher concluded that with rising costs he could no longer afford to print the book. The editors were left with a manuscript running to some thirteen thousand entries annotated to the specifications of one publisher, which specifications would probably not fit those of the next publisher. The moral seems to be that for great reference works, especially cooperative works, authors and editors are by nature interreliant.

Other books probably lie somewhere between a poem by Frost and a many-volumed reference work. Textbooks, in which I assume this group is interested, fall toward the middle somewhere, reflecting rather close association between author and representatives of the publisher. *Modern English Handbook,* which Robert M. Gorrell and I did, may serve as a case. Various publishers had suggested that one or the other of us might want to do a handbook; we decided that handbooks for composition were inevitably routine and dull, and we wanted none of them. The publishers persisted. I suggested to Gorrell that we prepare a prospectus for a book sufficiently startling so that nobody would dare publish it; then maybe somebody would be impressed enough to offer us something interesting. Several publishers wanted the book, and by this time, having discovered that editors are not nearly so impervious to ideas as we had supposed, we became excited about the possibility of a book which would teach writing positively. Now we had to weigh all kinds of imponderables: how permissive should one be? How much should we adopt the so-called "new grammars," and which ones? How could essentials be emphasized, by analysis, by synthesis, by eloquence, by sweet patience, or by what? And how does a student learn to write anyhow? Here we found that we were continually appealing to the representatives of the publisher whose offer we had accepted, both the people called editors and the people called salesmen. Eventually we produced a draft, which the editors commented upon and sent to various readers, who added more comments, most of them contradictory. Out of all this welter of statement and counter-statement, we redefined the book and rewrote it, after which it was edited again and went to press, with the authors and the publisher's editor proposing changes through galley proof and on into page proof.

So, at last, the book was out, but that was only the beginning. It did fairly well—better, as a matter of fact than we had expected— but the publisher's editor reported that it would sell much better if we could sharpen our treatment of usage. We had tried to please too many people, relying upon modern linguistics to make the liberals happy, but at the same time only enough prescriptive usage— as we hoped—to keep the conservatives from being too unhappy. The result was that liberals did not like the book enough, and conservatives were not jarred out of their conservatism anyhow. Accordingly, we now eschewed compromise, which we had not liked in any event, and tried to make the treatment of usage more consistent while enunciating for ourselves a principle which we have followed ever since—try to make a book that some people will like very much and don't worry about trying to please people who will never like your book anyhow. Subsequently other editions were called for, and each time in determining the general lines the revision should follow, we worked with various representatives of the publisher.

And this brings me to publisher's editors, of which there are various sorts, in general, I should say, three: what one might call contracting editors, development editors, and copyreading editors. A contracting editor—the most volatile and omnipresent examplar I know of is Bill Pullin—gets ideas for books, hears about ideas that other people have for books, knows people who might possibly write books, drafts and signs contracts, and forgets all about the author until the next NCTE convention, when the contracting editor encounters the author in a lobby and buys him a drink. Meanwhile, the development editor has taken over; he and the author work together more or less closely through the actual planning of the book, and continuing through its various drafts, of which there are usually at least two, and may be many. A good development editor does not try to write the author's book: he is rather like a midwife, who does not attempt to have the mother's baby for her, but does help the expectant mother bring to birth a baby that is already conceived. When the manuscript is essentially complete it goes to a copy editor, who styles the manuscript for the printer, but usually, also, pounces upon the less literate phrases and the more dubious pronouncements. Of course the functions of these various editors may overlap or even be rolled into one, but in big companies maid-of-all-work editors are rare.

Now before my time runs out let me say something of what editors and publishers are not. They are not dull-witted shysters trying to con brilliant but gullible authors out of their ideas. This notion is commonly abroad, that publishers will steal ideas and use them to write books with, or they will steal the manuscripts of beginning authors and use them to get rich. Theoretically, this sort of thing could happen, and in some areas it may, but practically speaking, not among reputable textbook publishers. Partly, publishers know that honesty is good business; even a whisper of chicanery would harm them; authors of textbooks are also adopters of textbooks and adopters are all potential authors. Furthermore, publishers know that ideas are not worth stealing, that no idea is any good to them unless somebody can write it; they know that no textbook is much good unless it can be attributed to reputable person. Thus I suspect—although I cannot know, for I am not a publisher—that in the eyes of a publisher the two worst crimes an editor can commit are these: to let a bad book get into print, and to let a good author get away. At least so far as I am concerned, editors have given me words, sentences, whole paragraphs; they did not even expect to be thanked, and they have never stolen anything.

Furthermore, most representatives of publishers are nice people; the kind of people who might otherwise be teachers, writers, librarians, artists—just the kind of people I, at least, like best; the kind of people who like books, and ideas, and other people. Of course publishers are business men; they may induce you to sign a contract that is not to your advantage, but once the contract is signed they are likely to be scrupulous in its observance and even generous in its interpretation. There are exceptions; editors are human beings, and there is a sort of natural enmity between editors and authors. Authors may think that editors are thwarted writers whom the Lord forgot to endow with brains, and editors may think that authors are thwarted beatniks whom the Lord forgot to endow with good sense, but on the whole, so far as I know, authors and editors tend to be pretty much the same sort of people, who may even develop fast friendships.

And since I have told you what editors are not, let me also hazard what authors are not. They are not plutocrats who toss off a book now and then and thereafter luxuriate in the royalties. On the whole they are people willing to work harder than do most of their colleagues, who take their vacations batting typewriters instead of golf balls; some of them are gamblers at heart but gamblers who would rather hazard their time than their money. They know that an author may make money, and they understandably hope they will make some, but they also know—or they soon find out—that most books make no money, or very little, for anybody except printers and purveyors of woodpulp. Most people who write books, whether textbooks or any other kind, write them for the best of reasons, because they want to write books. Of course no one can know, but personally I am convinced that books written mainly to make money do not usually make much, and hence when somebody asks me if he should not write textbooks to make a lot of money, I am tempted to suggest that he get a nice cushy job as baby sitter to a half dozen juvenile delinquent morons. He may live longer, and he will probably die wealthier.